ONE FAMILY UNDER HEAVEN
Response to Paradigm Shifts in Ecumenism

ONE FAMILY UNDER HEAVEN
Response to Paradigm Shifts in Ecumenism

JOSEPH DANIEL

ISPCK
2008

iv

ONE FAMILY UNDER HEAVEN: Response to Paradigm Shifts in Ecumenism – Published by the Rev. Dr. Ashish Amos of the Indian Society for Promoting Christian Knowledge (ISPCK), Post Box 1585, 1654, Madarsa Road, Kashmere Gate, Delhi-110006.

ISBN : 978-81-8458-055-6

Cover credit: Internet sources

Laser typeset by **ISPCK,** Post Box 1585, 1654, Madarsa Road, Kashmere Gate, Delhi-110006.
Tel: 23866322/23
e-mail– ashish@ispck.org.in • ella@ispck.org.in
website-www.ispck.org.in
Printed at Repro Knowledgecast Limited

CONTENTS

Foreword

I am delighted to write a foreword to the book, "**One Family Under Heaven**" authored by the Rev. Joseph Daniel. As the present Director of the Ecumenical Christian Centre, I would like to congratulate the author on the publication of the book and thank him for undertaking a study on the ECC.

The work was originally a Master of Theology degree thesis submitted to the Senate of Serampore University in February 2006. The book, as it is today, has undergone the needed revision which makes it a work of authority on the Ecumenical Christian Centre. The author has taken pains in consulting all the available source material pertaining to the centre right from its inception till the present, and hence it is the most up-to-date work on the Ecumenical Christian Centre.

The author is able to perceive very clearly the vision of the founder of the ECC, the late Rev. Dr. M.A.Thomas, and assess critically the contributions of the centre to humankind at different stages of its growth. Anyone interested in knowing about the ECC and its role in the ecumenical movement will find the work very rewarding. It is indeed my privilege to present the book to a wider readership.

<table>
<tr><td>Ecumenical Christian Centre
Post Bag 11, Whitefield
Bangalore – 560066.</td><td>**– Rev. Dr. M. Mani Chacko,**
PhD (London)
Director</td></tr>
</table>

Preface

The locus and paradigm of an ecumenical organisation evolve as the fusion of institutional horizons and an era's dominant episteme, discourses and practices churns out leaders with a definite flavour of the aesthetics, consciousness and values of a particular milieu. This is true of Rev. M.A. Thomas, who was born in 1913 as the son of a missionary and ventured into India's national freedom struggle and global ecumenical movements.

This book, "One Family Under Heaven", written by Rev. Joseph Daniel narrates an evolutionary story as it studies in detail the Ecumenical Christian Centre (ECC) in Whitefield, Bangalore – the history of its emergence through M.A. Thomas, who embodied the ecumenical vision of an era, and its development over the years.

There is no institution without community. An institution becomes an institution in relation to its larger community. It is in his or her community that a human being becomes really human. For the establishment, the multitude – community – is just outside of the agenda. However, a nurturing of a community is the ministry of the Church and ecumenical institutions. The book describes the work of the ECC in this regard.

The search for the "universal" in humans was the epistemic foundation of modernity, as Mahatma Gandhi reminded M.A. Thomas in a letter: "The best and most effective propaganda against the communal spirit is to express the 'universal' in our own lives."

The concept of modernity underscores the "universal" by implying that history is moving from parochial, ethnic, tribal, religious and caste enclaves towards a universal humanity in which all humans are fundamentally equal. "All men are created equal." The "universal" pertains to values, human rights, freedoms, culture, and democracy.

It is important here to underline the oneness of the Church – its Christo-centricity and catholicity – as well as the concept of the "universal". Ecumenism is not an arena where we water down differences, but it's where we pool together resources. Ecumenism is not about agreeing on the minimum on which all people can come together, but it's about sharing the riches of the common heritage of all creation.

Organisations like the Students' Christian Movement, the International Missionary Conference and the World Council of Churches, all share one vision – of uniting humankind by bringing in discourses of peace and harmony in different historical settings. In the 1930s, the concern of ecumenical gatherings was the Church, but in the '60s, the unity of humankind became the theme of discussion and practice.

Rev. Joseph Daniel has quoted the keynote address delivered by the late Mar Thoma Metropolitan, Juhanon Mar Thoma at the general assembly of the World Council of Churches in 1961, in New Delhi. That speech was essentially a call to take seriously the issues of the "secular world". The New Delhi WCC assembly stressed that "there was no separate existence of the Church without addressing the general problems of the world. Hence, the Church had to take the world and its historical events seriously".

The deliberations of the second Vatican Council (1962-65) also shared the same concerns.

The Ecumenical Christian Centre, which was instituted in 1963 with Rev. M.A. Thomas as its founding director, consolidated the aspirations and vision of the vibrant ecumenical movement of that century.

Rev. Daniel notes ECC's guiding principles thus: "There was a genuine attempt to translate the basic philosophy of the centre, 'wider ecumenism', into its concerns, awareness and action plans. The centre was true to its four basic thrusts, namely the unity of churches (healing of the divisions in the body of Christ), the unity of faiths (search for theological understanding of other faiths), the unity and renewal of humankind (discovery of authentic options for the healing of human brokenness) and the integrity of creation (maintaining a caring attitude towards all living beings)."

The dawn of the 20th Century saw the emergence of the ecumenical movement, which stood for the unity of Christian missions of different denominations and thereby the unity of churches, but also had economic developmental issues and the unity of humankind, questions of justice and peace, the necessity of dialogue between people of other faiths, ecological concerns and the very question of "life" among its pertinent concerns. Presently, post-modern paradigms challenge ecumenical thinkers to ignore the "differences" in human communities and look to form a community of communities in the new millennium. Rev Daniel has attempted to clearly bring out the actions and thrusts of the ECC in this direction.

Institutions like ECC and people like Rev. M.A. Thomas have become signposts that have illuminated the history of ecumenism in its leap towards forging a human existence marked by dialogue and sharing in the secular space.

This is a resurrection experience too. Resurrection is a process of transformation of our relationships. The book challenges us to commit ourselves to the search for that abundant and resurrected life.

Rev. Joseph Daniel, a priest in the Mar Thoma Church, has been a very good student of history and theology. His wealth of historical knowledge comes through in this book, as also his insight, borne of keen and painstaking research into ECC's history.

He has presented the different thrusts of the ecumenical movement over the years and has tried to draw their parallels in ECC's own history in an intelligible and relevant manner.

I am happy to commend him on this work.

– Philipose Mar Chrysostom
MAR THOMA VALIYA METROPOLITAN

1

Seeds of Wider Ecumenism

The Ecumenical Christian Centre at Whitefield can be said to be the fulfillment of my dreams. All my activities in different streams of life up to my 50th year – participation and role in the international and ecumenical conferences and contacts with ecumenical leaders, the craving for the unity of the churches and the entire humanity, and, above all, my obedience to Christ – all these, the channels along which my life and thinking had travelled and struggled, contributed their share to the making of this experiment.

– M. A. Thomas, in his book, *A Leap Into The Unknown,* on the factors that inspired him to found the Ecumenical Christian Centre (ECC), Whitefield, Bangalore.

BORN on 10th August, 1913, in a middle class family at Muvattupuzha in Kerala, mission was in M. A. Thomas' blood – his father, M. C. Abraham, was the first missionary of the Mar Thoma Church in North Travancore.

His training and upbringing did play a part in shaping his mission, which was to further the cause of ecumenism. Thomas had his early education in a government primary school at Valakom, in Quilon district of Kerala, and later at the St. Thomas English Medium Middle School, Keezhillam,

Kerala. He once recalled in an interview how teachers of the St. Thomas school had instilled in him Christian disciplines, such as morning and evening prayers and Bible reading, and had taught him the importance of self-reliance. Among his teachers there was the late Mathews Mar Athanasius Episcopa of the Mar Thoma Church.

After getting his B.A. degree, Thomas wrote to the Church Secretary, expressing his desire to be ordained as a priest of the Mar Thoma Church. There was a delay in the Church's reply to him and this gave Thomas a chance to get himself involved in the Students' Christian Movement (SCM) as a secretary for Madras and Vellore areas. Later, he joined Westcott House in the United Kingdom for theological studies.

On his return from Cambridge after the completion of his studies, Thomas was ordained deacon on 14th January, 1950, by Juhanon Mar Thoma Metropolitan and, three months later, as a priest. Later, Thomas was to reminisce how the visionary and ecumenist in Juhanon Mar Thoma guided and encouraged him to continue on his ecumenical pursuits. The training and upbringing that Thomas received as a member of the Mar Thoma Church and later as a priest were factors that firmed his ecumenical resolve.

RESULT OF OBEDIENCE

Thomas always stressed that it was his obedience to God's calling and guidance that was a major impetus in his search of ecumenism. The founding of ECC was a result of this obedience, he would say. A major motivating factor behind this obedience was his great dream of a wider unity, which, in turn, was the result of his wide range of contacts with secular and religious organisations.

In Thomas' own words:

"The idea of 'one family under heaven' has been growing in me since the days of the 'Inter-Religious Students' Fellowship'. On certain occasions, I had to struggle with other forces, weaning me away from this central idea. Ultimately the idea, 'one family under heaven' won the battle. To me that meant obedience to Christ."

ECC was, therefore, the flowering of a sincere search for a new style of Christian obedience to the challenges posed by the socio-political and ecumenical realms. The main driving force behind this was the commitment of Thomas to the fullness of humanity and obedience to Christ.

However, his zeal for wider unity had been evident much earlier. In one instance, just after his marriage on 7th November, 1940, Thomas served food to some people of Kerala's lower castes at the same table where upper-caste "St. Thomas Christians" also sat – in open defiance of the social norms then prevalent. Thomas, who belonged to the tradition of the "St. Thomas Christians", showed caste barriers within the social system could be transcended.

The importance of such actions cannot be underestimated especially when viewed against history. Prior to the Synod of Diamper (1599), there were no external signs in the social life of St. Thomas Christians to distinguish them from the Hindu community in Kerala. They followed the same social practices prevalent during the milieu, when upper caste Christians looked down upon their lower caste brethren, who were considered "untouchables."

But the Synod of Diamper forbade a number of customs and practices, which the Portuguese considered pagan (Hindu). These prohibitions and restrictions imposed by the synod had a bearing on the communal harmony and cordial relations that existed between Christians and Hindus.

CHAMPIONING THE CAUSE OF AMITY

This issue of how Christians should relate to people of other faith had in fact been a concern since the beginning of the modern ecumenical movement. Thomas worked for social amity among the Hindus – urging for a greater social interplay between the lower and upper castes.

He was to take these efforts to a new theological level later by bringing in all sections of the Indian society – irrespective of caste, colour, religion, gender, and so on – to participate in the activities of ECC with a view to further his ultimate dream of "one world family under heaven."

Thomas, in fact, had a unique field of experience as he had been actively associated, as a teenager, with Hindu and Muslim friends in the All Kerala Balajana Sakhyam, a children's forum organised under the aegis of the *Malayala Manorama* newspaper. He had also been active in the Inter-Religious Student Fellowship of India, Youth Christian Council of Action and Students' Christian Movement of India (SCM).

During his high-school days, Thomas took the initiative to form branches of the Balajana Sakhyam and won a silver medal for enrolling the largest number of members. He proved his leadership abilities in the Balajana Sakhyam, where he was elected as secretary unanimously in 1930. This phase in his life helped him see the ground realities of the people and to develop an idea of wider unity.

His involvement with the Indian freedom struggle was another platform in his pursuit of wider unity. During the *Nivarthana Prasthanam, a Socio-religious* action movement of those years, backward caste Ezhavas, Muslims and Christians had joined hands to fight social inequality. This provoked the upper-caste Nair community to turn against the Christians. Thomas wanted to nip this problem in the bud and wrote to Mahatma Gandhi, asking him how this problem could be combated. Gandhi replied:

> *"The best and most effective propaganda against the communal spirit is to express the universal in our own lives."*

These words continued to echo within Thomas. In 1935, he was elected as the secretary of the university wing of the International fellowship, an Indian movement for inter-religious cooperation and national integration, which held its biennial conference in Wardha, India.

In his own words, Thomas accepted the post "on the basis that a follower of any religion could become a member of the fellowship without compromising on one's faith." This opened a new field of work to integrate people of other faiths in the common cause of India and to rally people of all religions against rigid fundamentalism and proselytism.

Along the way, a concept of wider unity – that neither advocates the negation of one's faith and belief nor the exclusion of any one from the unity umbrella, but advocates mutual respect – took root in Thomas' mind.

Institutionalising this concept became Thomas' dream. His association with the SCM and a sojourn in Cambridge, where he established close contact with leaders like Cecil Hargreaves, Bishop Oliver S Tompkins, Reinhold Neibubr and so on helped provide a theological grounding for this dream. Besides, he attended a number of world conferences, including the 1947 World Conference of the Youth held under the auspices of the World Council of Churches (WCC) in Oslo. These exposures widened the horizon of his friendship and understanding of wider unity and helped him to have a desire for an *ashram*-like institution.

2

Paradigm Changes

... 'Ecumenical' is not specifically a Christian word, although it is generally used to refer to the world-wide movement for inter-church co-operation and Church unity. It has .... a wider meaning pertaining to the unity of humanity and the whole inhabited world and its concerns. This covers the socio-economic and political concerns of all people. The struggle of the oppressed people for justice is, therefore, an ecumenical concern.

*– **M. A. Thomas** reflects on ecumenism in an interview*

The ecumenical movement has become an important principle in the life of the Church, and it was particularly so during the 20th century. Since 1950 the movement has called for a wider understanding of the meaning of ecumenism — with regard to the Church and, in wider terms, in relation to humankind as a whole.

This is well-reflected above in the words of Thomas. The word, ecumenism, has a wider meaning that implies the unity of all humankind, the inhabited world and its concerns. Having been influenced by this fervour, Thomas dreamed of an appropriate institution to impart awareness and education on his vision to all communities in India and abroad. As his vision of wider unity and WCC's articulations on ecumenism converged, this dream certainly had strong foundations.

The concept of ecumenism has been evolving over the years, since the ecumenical movement had its formal inauguration in the 1910 World Missionary Conference in Edinburgh. In fact, the movement went through a series of "paradigm" shifts.

The term, paradigm, as defined in Thomas S Kuhn's work, *"The Structures of Scientific Revolution"*, stands for the entire constellation of beliefs, values, techniques and so on shared by members of a given community. The term, which has been taken from the debate on the development of scientific knowledge, is used to describe a situation of transition.

EVOLUTION OF ECUMENISM

The major thrust of most of the deliberations on mission in the 19th century was the unity of mission agencies. The idea then was to form a global Christian community with a view to bringing all mankind under it. Missionsinspecktor, Axenfeld, of the Berlin Missionary Society opines:

> *"...There shall not be any difference of opinion among the participants of the World Missionary Conference that 'we are not entered with merely spreading Christian civilization, to give to the foreign nations a superficial Christian-like tinge. We wish to bring single hearts into real and everlasting personal communion with the everlasting God'."*

In the period between 1910 and the late 1960s, the meaning of the ecumenical movement widened from the unity of churches and mission societies to the unity of all human beings. This major change came about as a result of the shifts of emphasis in ecumenical discussions and its practice. In the 1930s, the Church became the locus of mission.

But by the 1950s, a paradigm shift resulted in the world becoming a major area of the Church's activity, and by 1968, the unity of humankind became the agenda of the ecumenical movement.

The general assumption of the Edinburgh Conference was mission from the West to the East – the West then being understood as Christian and the East "un-Christian." The Western Church then considered itself as the custodian of Christian spirituality and as the provider of Christian teachings. The mission societies from the West took upon themselves the task to convert the "un-Christian" East. In simple words, the West became the "provider" and the East the "receiver."

It was then conveniently forgotten that missions originated from the Church and were under the Church. They took a life of their own. Meanwhile, a tendency grew for the mission societies to look down upon the mission fields, where natives were converted to Christianity and new churches were formed. The Western missionaries then termed the new entities "younger churches" against their own established ones, which they considered "older."

There was much discussion during the late 1920s on the relationship between the "younger and older" churches. There was also an obvious concern reflected in these debates on the question of the centrality and authority of the Church as against the mission societies. The 1938 International Missionary Council (IMC) meeting at Tambaram, in Madras, brought out the Church's central role in mission. Ecumenical thinker William Richy Hogg talks about this in his book, *Ecumenical Foundations:*

> *"Madras made the Church its central concern and a new sense of its reality ran through every statement produced there. As never before had been possible, the members of churches saw the Church universal partially disclosed in their midst. In a day*

when many regarded the historic Church as an unnecessary appendage to "the Christian spirit", Madras brought a new awareness of the Church's importance."

The formation of IMC in 1921, the Life and Work Movement in 1925, and the Faith and Order Movement in 1927 did provide support to the Church being hoisted on to the focal point of mission. These three movements culminated in the founding of the World Council of Churches (WCC). Another major historical development was the socio-political situation precipitated by the First World War (1914-1918). This opened the eyes of ecumenical leaders to the need for social service, which eventually came to be regarded as part and parcel of mission work.

This further resulted in the Church examining mission in the light of issues prevalent in mission societies and also under the socio-political situations such as the Great Depression (1929-32) and the Second World War (1939-45). The ecumenical leaders then realised the need for an overarching umbrella body for the churches to coordinate the work of the IMC, the Life and Work Movement and the Faith and Order Movement.

The result was the formation of the World Council of Churches (WCC) in 1948.

FROM 'CHURCH-CENTRIC' TO 'WORLD-CENTRIC'

It was against this background that another major shift in emphasis started making its presence felt in the ecumenical movement. This was the development of new ideas such as "partnership in obedience" and "partnership in mission" that took world realities seriously and found that mission could not be separated from the world and its realities. These ideas formed the core of the discussions at the 1947 IMC conference in Ontario, Canada.

In 1952, the IMC conference at Willingen, Germany, in a report titled *"The Missionary Obligation of the Church"*, emphasised the need for the Church to be in solidarity with the world. It says:

> *"This word, "witness", cannot possibly mean that the Church stands over against the world, detached from it and regarding it from a position of superior righteousness or security. The Church is in the world. As the Lord of the Church identified Himself wholly with mankind, so must the Church also do. The nearer the Church draws to its Lord, the nearer it draws to the world. Christians do not live in an enclave separated from the world; they are God's people in the world."*

This was a major shift of emphasis towards a "world-centric mission" in ecumenical thinking. The basis of this emphasis was the Hebrew understanding of God and history, according to which God had absolute control over *cosmos* and He was thus the Lord of history. Along with this came the thinking that being involved in events and movements in history was part of mission.

AS GOD ACTS IN HISTORY ...

All this was happening as the world was witnessing a period of tumultuous changes in its socio-political history. Many of the Asian, African and Latin American countries had just experienced freedom from foreign domination and they had entered into a struggle for justice and peace in their living situations. In India, it was the first decade of the post-Independence era that saw the country embarking on five-year plans for economic development.

Welfare of all, irrespective of socio-religious and political positions, had started gaining currency during this period in all new nation states. Moreover, the philosophy of modernity, as the great eighteenth century philosopher, Immanuel Kant, had propounded, was becoming popular. This led to new forms of moral theology and forced thinkers of the time and ecumenists to identify issues involved in the fields of human justice and peace.

The articulation of ecumenism's new emphasis on the secular world was the result of the reflections of theologians Dietrich Bonhoeffer, J.C. Hoekendijk, M.M. Thomas and others, who made concerted attempts to take the secular world seriously in their thinking.

Protestant theologian, Bonhoeffer, in his *"Letters and Papers from Prison"*, said the world that was coming of age was more godless and, perhaps for that reason, nearer to God than the world earlier. For Bonhoeffer, to live in Christ meant to be a Church that existed not for the pious and the faithful but for others. In Bonhoeffer's view, the only concept of God appropriate to a religionless Christian faith is that of God in his powerlessness and suffering for others in crucifixion.

In Bonhoeffer's words:

Our relation to God is not a religious relationship to a Supreme Being, absolute in power and goodness, which is a spurious conception of transcendence, but a new life for others, through participation in the Being of God. The transcendence consists not in tasks beyond our scope and power, but in the nearest thing to hand God in human form ... man existing for others and hence the crucified."

– **Dietrich Bonhoeffer:** *"Prisoner of God"*

What Bonhoeffer affirmed was that the world and the secular culture in which people carried out daily tasks were legitimate concerns of Christians. This, in turn, disclosed a new interest in the historical Jesus as the paradigm of worldly transcendence. It is this vision of worldly secular Christianity that has been shared by a large number of theologians since the 1960s.

M. M. Thomas, a noted Indian theologian, politician and a close friend of M. A. Thomas, made it clear that both Church and the world had the same centre, which was Jesus Christ. In the book, *"My Ecumenical Journey"*, he held the view that there was no separate existence for the Church apart from this world. The Church had no distinct and separate sphere of activity from this world and its history.

M.M. Thomas' theological emphasis thus stressed the world and history. The earlier premise of the church being against the world had been replaced by the concept of mission being rooted in the world. This paradigm shift, which was further reflected in the works of other noted theologians, was the focus in the discussions of the third WCC general assembly in New Delhi, in 1961.

As mentioned earlier, the WCC was formed in 1948. Its first general assembly in Amsterdam, the second in Evanston (1954) and the third in New Delhi (1961) provided a progression of ecumenical witness in the world. In Amsterdam, the churches expressed their desire to "stay together". In Evanston, they expressed their desire to "grow together". In New Delhi, besides emphasising ecumenism, witness and service, the WCC stressed the significance of local unity, using the phrase, "in each place", to drive this idea.

CHRIST IN TIMES OF DESPAIR AND DARKNESS

In Evanston and New Delhi, WCC focused on the post-war condition in the world and the intensity of the darkness prevailing globally. The New Delhi assembly, emphasised the need for the redemptive message of Christ to be communicated to the world of despair and darkness through service, unity and witness. This included the reconstruction of society.

In his presidential address during the general session in New Delhi, Juhanon Mar Thoma Metropolitan set the tone for the WCC general assembly by focusing on the need for the Church to respond positively to the problems of the prevailing milieu. The summary of the session clearly conveys a shift of emphasis in ecumenical vision and thinking. These were its recommendations:

1. *Facilitate identification with the whole humanity.*

2. *Give impetus and content to the development of an international ethos.*

3. *Fashion a witness, which is unaligned with any political or national force but committed to peace with justice and freedom.*

4. *Encourage the building of an 'open society' throughout the world.*

5. *Assist in defining opportunities for peaceful cooperation as a means of living together in a divided world.*

6. *Give a prominent place to the claims of social justice for all men everywhere.*

These points from New Delhi reflect the importance of the "secular" in the ecumenical discussions. They emphasised that there was no separate existence of the Church without addressing the general problems of the world. Hence the Church had to take the world and its historical events seriously. The ecumenical movement's rediscovery of the world as the locus of its existence was thus also a key moment in the history of the Church and the world.

ONUS ON THE INDIAN CHURCH

New Delhi marked a radical shift of focus in the ecumenical movement, says Collin W Williams, in his book, *"New Directions in Theology Today: The Church."* In an article titled *"Ecumenicals and Evangelicals – a Grouping Relationship?"* in the journal, *The Ecumenical Review*, David J Bosch says New Delhi "inaugurated a new era in the conciliar movement. Until then, it was the Church that received most attention in the Council's deliberations, henceforth it would be the world".

M. A. Thomas himself was aware about the importance of the New Delhi assembly and expressed his indebtedness to it for the launch of the ECC project. In his Malayalam book, *"Ormakaliloode" (Down Memory Lane)*, Thomas says:

> *"That this event of supreme importance in Christian history has taken place in India, predominantly a country with different faiths, puts the Indian Church under a special obligation to stand firmly behind the great act of God. The South Indian ecumenical institution, which will now come into being, shall be a commemorative institution of this great historic event ..."*

These words clearly bring out not just the influence contemporary ecumenical thinking had on Thomas, they also showed his resolve to give shape to his ecumenical vision in "south Indian ecumenical institution" that would offer a meeting place for all humanity.

WIDER ECUMENISM – IN THE CATHOLIC CHURCH

A similar development was making waves in the Catholic circles – almost simultaneously – as the second Vatican

Council opened its windows to not just other Christians, but also to people of other faiths. The path taken by the Roman Catholic Church after the first Vatican Council of 1870, by affirming the infallibility of the Pope and the condemnation of modernism, had kept away other Christians and people of other faiths from its thinking and spirituality. However, John XXIII's ascent to the Papal throne in 1958 was about to change all that.

On 25th January, 1959, Pope John XXIII announced his plan to summon an ecumenical council of the Church. The second Vatican Council that opened in 1962 was a defining moment for the Catholic Church and its ecumenical thinking. Christian thinker, Robert McAfee Brown describes its impact thus:

> *The second Vatican Council (1962-1965) ended outside St. Peter's on a beautifully sunny day, with the Church offering itself as the servant of the world – a theme that will increasingly unite Roman Catholicism, not only with the rest of Christendom but with all men of goodwill.*

The second Vatican Council also accepted the collegiality of bishops, the active implementation of which would involve a reformation of the Church and open the way for a deepening ecumenical dialogue with other churches and even people of other faiths.

Besides, the "Decree on Ecumenism", a document presented at the second Vatican Council, was one of paramount importance, because for the first time in the Catholic Church after reformation, the decree accepted the non-Catholic Christian communities in its ecclesiastical sense. The second Vatican Council and the 1961 WCC assembly in New Delhi contributed much to a newfound desire for closer ties between the churches. This desire was another force that influenced the thinking of M.A. Thomas that eventually led to the envisioning of an institution for the cause of wider ecumenism.

IN INDIA, A NEW PHASE BEGINS

In the post-Independence Indian scenario, nationalism, nation-building, development and social justice came to the fore for the Church and its mission after 1960. The struggle for independence and the subsequent process of nation-building opened a new arena of activity to the Church with regard to its life and witness in the field of social, political and cultural settings.

Besides, the theologians affirmed that Christ is present in world realities. This resulted in the formation of charitable institutions and hospitals by the Church in various parts of the country by different denominations.

A change was felt in the perspectives of Christian witness aimed at achieving development based on justice and service. It was in this context that the Indian Church rendered pioneering service by setting up medical and educational institutions in large-scale as well as charitable institutions like orphanages and starting relief operations through Christian Agency for Social Action (CASA) to meet the needs of the Indian society as a whole without any religious or racial discrimination.

This marked the beginning of a new phase of activity in the Indian Church as it started developmental projects with the help of foreign donor agencies. This mission was aimed at creating infrastructure for community development in all areas of life and to equip the poor and needy in the society for self-reliance in their life. Thus the Indian Church realised the fact that witness was possible only in solidarity with people and their struggles. This opened a new window of wider unity of all humanity in the ecclesiastical and ecumenical realms.

However, such charitable and developmental activities seldom challenged the existing structure of injustice that perpetuated poverty and unequal distribution of wealth and resources. By this time, the influence of liberation theology that was applied in the Latin American struggles for social justice had also found its echo in the Indian ecumenical and mission context. This led to the awareness that the struggle for justice was also God's mission.

Such a thinking demanded a common meeting place for all Christians and people of other faiths to share their common concerns on society and the nation. This would indirectly help to foster wider unity and nation building as well as equipping them to challenge existing social structures.

Having realised the pulse of the time, M. A. Thomas took it is a challenge.

3
Building up on a Vision

Every one of us is part of the continent, part of the mainland
Not one of us is an island
We are men and women, of one world household
Participating together in the life of the mainland
In our family,
Our community,
Our community of nations,
We are not … none of us … an island

> — **M. A. Thomas**, in his book, *About You and Me*

The above words by Thomas provide a picture that he yearned to communicate all through his life – that no man is an island to himself, but part of the larger created order. Each man's or woman's mission, Thomas wanted the world to know, is to be a responsible world citizen and to join other fellow human beings to strive for the good of humanity wherever God has placed him or her.

Ecumenism, in Thomas' view, had ceased to be a concept that merely stood for the unity of all churches. On the contrary, it was a worldview that stood for a wider unity – of all human kind and also in our relationship with the earth.

A DREAM SLOWLY TAKES SHAPE

ECC, as we saw in the first two chapters, was the result of the vision and longing of Thomas for that "one world family under heaven." More significantly, it was the result of his humble obedience to a divine challenge to bring all those vulnerable people outside the purview of unity under the wider ecumenical umbrella. And, his deep concern for ecumenical action gave expression to a clear vision through his experiences in India and abroad.

It would then only be a matter of time before bricks and mortar could provide a concrete shape to a man's dream to take wider ecumenism from the conceptual realm to reality.

Still, it was no cakewalk.

It was in 1960, when Thomas was serving as a vicar of the Mar Thoma Church in Madras, that the paradigm shift in ecumenism started appealing to the ecumenist in him to do something concrete about it. The dream was to build a centre for wider ecumenism.

The main aim of the centre would be to provide an ecumenical forum for all churches in India to come together and be benefited by the fellowship. Thomas prepared a detailed plan in 1961 and shared it with his friends. A budget of about Rs1.6 million was also prepared.

In the same year, Thomas attended the WCC general assembly in New Delhi, having received an invitation from Daniel Thambyrajah Niles, an ecumenical leader from Sri Lanka, and an ordained priest of the Methodist Church. Niles had taken a prominent role at the IMC conference in Tambaram and was also chairman of WCC'S youth department during 1948-'52 and executive secretary of WCC's department of evangelism during 1953-'59.

MOBILISING SUPPORT

The main intention of Thomas' Delhi visit was to discuss the plan for the centre with a close friend, P. D. Devanadan, who had co-founded, with Dr. M.M. Thomas, the Christian Institute for the Study of Religion and Society (CISRS), a pioneering study centre in India in 1957. CISRS was involved in wide-ranging studies, research and inter-faith dialogue, but also appealed to churches to participate actively in the process of building a just society in India.

Thomas' idea somehow did not strike a chord with Devanadan, who was not enthused by the huge financial commitment that the centre entailed. Nevertheless, Thomas was not disheartened.

After all, it was not a fruitless journey. In New Delhi, Thomas was able to get the support and sympathy for the project from stalwarts like Niles, prominent theologian J. R. Chandran, a former principal of the United Theological College, Bangalore; Oliver Tomkins, former bishop of England; Juhanon Mar Thoma, Philipose Mar Chrysostom, former metropolitans of the Mar Thoma Church. That further steeled Thomas' resolve.

In 1962, when the Mar Thoma Church transferred Thomas to Bangalore as the vicar of the Primrose Road Church, he was to find further support from the Christian leadership there. Prominent among them were Chandran himself and E. V. Mathew, a lawyer in the High Court of Karnataka and an ecumenist who had participated in the third general assembly of the WCC in New Delhi. A few serious consultations with church leaders followed.

A meeting of the leaders representing various national churches and organisations met for one full day on 5th January, 1963, at the parish hall of St. Mark's Cathedral, Bangalore, under the chairmanship of Chandran. Thomas presented the plan for a centre, but could not show the source of funds.

That meeting resolved:

> *"… to establish the Ecumenical Center in Bangalore and appoint a director, not knowing how or from where the finances would come either for the setting up of the center or for the support of its workers. The metropolitan of the Mar Thoma Church was requested to kindly lend the services of M. A. Thomas to be the first director of the centre."*

> – **ECC:** *Report of the Executive Committee to the Governing Council, 18th April, 1964*

Thus, on 5th January, 1963, the Ecumenical Christian Center (ECC) was founded under the chairmanship of J. R. Chandran, with M. A. Thomas as its founder director. The episcopal synod of the Mar Thoma Church had given consent to M. A. Thomas to take responsibility as the director of ECC, with effect from 1st May, 1963.

As the vicar of Primrose Road Church, Thomas stayed at a rented house in Cox Town, Bangalore. A small room at the parsonage was converted as the ECC's office. The first office of the ECC had just enough space to accommodate two tables and two chairs. A secretary was appointed on a monthly salary of Rs 8. Thomas was to write about this later in *Ormakaliloode* (Down Memory Lane):

> *"… it marked the beginning of an adventurous and hazardous journey with just the wide world in front of me, least bothered whether it would end in success or failure …"*

Membership in the ECC by major mainland churches of India followed.

INVESTING IN FAITH

At the St. Mark's Cathedral meeting, which was the first governing council meeting of the ECC, Thomas presented a Rs1.6 million budget for the centre, but had no funds whatsoever. What Thomas had, however, was a deep faith that "the great God is above and the wide world is around", as the ECC founder was to report later in his book, "*A Leap into the Unknown.*"

The God that promised faith can move mountains worked the same day as members who attended the meeting came out with Rs10 contributions, the first of which came from NC Sergeant, a bishop of the Church of South India (CSI).

The Governing Council also referred the proposal for the centre to the National Council of Churches in India (NCCI) and other ecumenical institutions for financial assistance. NCCI responded positively, with certain suggestions to reduce the budget for the centre. The ECC executive committee did scale down the budget to Rs400,000 from Rs1.6 million with an understanding that the centre would try and raise funds from friends through special efforts. It was also decided that the ECC would collect Rs100,000 within India itself in the first four years.

Thomas' wide circle of friends strengthened his hand as he visited different parts of India for financial support. And, in October, 1963, the NCCI recommended the ECC project for funding from the Inter-Church Aid of the WCC.

M. A. Thomas says:

"When we took the decision to establish the center, we had no funds at all. It looked like foolishness to the wise. Both in our country and abroad, there were expressions of anxiety and several well-meaning friends raised doubts whether the / Center would become an accomplished fact. However, we went ahead in faith and our faith has been amply rewarded. Not that we have plenty of money, but God has given us our daily bread. At every step, divine help was with us ..."

– **ECC**: *Report of the Executive Committee to the Governing Council, 10th April, 1964*

With this faith, Thomas approached several agencies and their financial support made his dream for a centre for wider ecumenism a reality.

FAITH STARTS TO BEAR FRUIT ...

Thomas located a vacant property of 18 acres that included a dilapidated house at Whitefield, about 20 km away from Bangalore city, for housing the ECC. Having received the mandate from the executive committee, the plot was bought on 27th June, 1964, for Rs 80,000.

Along with his young friend, M. J. Joseph, a student at the United Theological College, Bangalore, Thomas spent a night at the site. Joseph, an ecumenist himself and an ordained priest of the Mar Thoma church, was to later become the director of the ECC. It was a night the two savoured and meditated over the way the Almighty was bringing into fruition a vision to further the cause of wider unity. Joseph related this experience to this author in an interview on 27th June, 2005.

Later, 10 acres of land were added to the plot and buildings were constructed in a period of physical growth for the ECC from 1964 to 1972. J.M. Stevens, a priest of the Catholic Church, was the architect for the buildings.

The office of the ECC was shifted to the new building in 1967.

That the formation of the ECC was the result of a convergence of changes that occurred in ecumenical and theological thinking should be emphasised here. It became a reality when the visionary and ecumenist in Thomas, responded to these changes and acted in faith and in obedience to a calling from God – at a time when the whole world was focused on unity and welfare of all mankind in terms of kingdom values.

ECC, as Thomas then envisioned, was to serve as a place for all churches in India to come together, live together and involve in discussions with a view to understand one another better. This, in turn, would lead to a greater acceptance of each other.

4

Articulating Wider Ecumenism

Lord:

The demolition of walls between nations and races,

The banishment of barriers of religions and castes,

The obliteration of ghettoes among cultures and classes,

The extinction of hate between black and white

– is this not the breakthrough Lord,

– is this not your mission in the world,

      Our divided world?

          – M. A. Thomas: *About You and Me*

The first 50 years since the inception of the ecumenical movement in 1910 saw mission keeping the Church in its focus. Initially, the aim of all ecumenical endeavours was to shape the global Christian community.

However, the next 20 years saw the ecumenical movement discovering the world as its locus of life and activity. The study of the Bible, socio-religious factors and close contact with people of other faiths, cultures and ideologies convinced the stalwarts of the movement that Christians could no longer continue to look inwards.

This meant that the kingdom of God could not be limited to the expressions of the Christian community alone. The concerns of ecumenism had to be wider – one that involved justice, peace and integrity concerns of all creation.

But this thought trend was to come much later. Before the Tambaram IMC meeting, the attitude of missions towards other faiths was negative and even uncompromisingly hostile. Mission societies existed to conquer the people from different religious backgrounds and just did not recognize the right of other religions to exist.

A NEW APPROACH

But as always, God acted in history. The socio-political situation and the spread of new ideologies of nationalism after the 1950s necessitated a new approach in the evangelical task. In the 1954 Evanston WCC general assembly, it was accepted that the first step in evangelism "must always be not that of controversy but of identification and alongsideness." The 1961 New Delhi assembly, as mentioned earlier, emphasised the need for the redemptive message of Christ to be communicated to a world of darkness and despair through service.

This attitude of the WCC further developed in the Commission of World Mission and Evangelism Conference in Kandy in 1967, which marked the beginning of WCC's interest in dialogue with the people of other faiths in a significant way. In 1971, the WCC constituted a sub-unit called Dialogue with the People of Living Faiths and Ideologies. The idea of a world community became a major theme in the sub-unit's discussion.

In 1974, a conference of the sub-unit in Colombo discussed in depth the need for resources and for shouldering responsibilities in the building up of a harmonious world community and recognised the inter-dependence of people all over the world. These thrusts of the ecumenical leaders, the conference noted, should express in the socio-cultural, political and economic realms and contribute to a just and participatory world society that exists in a religiously harmonious setting. Thus WCC sought relations between people of different faiths to build new forms of collective life, as expressed in the Nairobi assembly in 1975.

Along the way, the Uppsala assembly of the WCC in 1968 had emphasised that ecumenism need not be unicoloured and static, but could connote a unity that is multi-coloured and diversified, or a "dynamic catholicity" that gave leeway for varying Christian lifestyles and witness. Uppsala emphasised the universal dimension of Church unity in these words:

> *"... a truly universal, ecumenical, conciliar form of common life and witness."*
>
> – **WCC:** *Official report of the Fourth Assembly of the WCC*

Thus the WCC Uppsala assembly envisaged the advent of a visible unity of the Church as a harbinger of a forthcoming unity of the whole mankind. What was visualised was not just the unity of different Christian denominations, but something that transcended issues like sex, race, class, caste, religion and whatever segregating human beings from each other.

WATERSHEDS

The 1975 Nairobi assembly went a step further to bring out more clearly the concept of "conciliar fellowship." In fact, Nairobi sought to break the existing barriers with people of other faiths. It recognised the fact that even if all Christians come together as one community, it could still be a minority.

It was in Nairobi that the Church expressly declared that seeking a community beyond Christianity was necessary for the sake of justice and peace and opened the doors for inter-religious dialogue. It was hoped that the new emphasis would help in establishing a just, participatory and sustainable society.

This thought trend was taken forward in Vancouver, where the WCC assembly in 1983 accepted that Christians live in a religiously and ideologically pluralistic world. The assembly recognised this fact in its statement with the following words:

> "... witness is not a one-way process from us to them. There is also a witness from them to us ...
>
> "... the concern for justice, peace and integrity of creation is not superficially 'Christian' concerns only ...
>
> "... the Biblical vision of peace with justice for all, of wholeness, of unity for all, is not one of several options of the followers of Christ. It is imperative in our times ..."
>
> – **WCC:** *Official Report of VI Assembly of World Council of Churches*

Thus, Vancouver stressed the need for an experience towards common action and cooperation between Christians and persons of other faiths. It emphasised the urgency of working together, especially for the upliftment of the poor and the needy, and to provide for all basic human dignity, justice, peace, economic reconstruction and the eradication of hunger and disease. So by this time, justice, peace and human rights concerns were also taken as part of Christian mission. These concerns were, after all, not just Christian concerns and were areas where there could be substantial joint endeavours.

The Canberra Assembly of the WCC in 1991 took a new approach. It considered the issues of justice, peace and the integrity of creation in the perspective of the Holy Spirit, the "giver of life" and the "spirit of truth." Moreover, it emphasised that man has to maintain the existence of the ecological system and should have the wisdom and humility to obey the laws of nature. Canberra also recognised the importance of the Holy Spirit in reviving life and in liberating people and communities from destructive tendencies. It solemnised a new commitment to justice, peace and the integrity of creation with the suffering world.

The assembly had been convened against the backdrop of the increasing recognition of an ecological crisis being perpetrated by man's excessive use of the soil that was leading to disappearing forest cover and depleting water supplies. Canberra recognised that an authentic relationship between human beings and between man and the non-human was a must for the survival of humanity.

RESPONDING TO GLOBALISATION

The 1998 eighth WCC general assembly held in Harare also acknowledged cultural and religious plurality as enduring features of human society, besides affirming a life-centred vision as it discussed the theme, "Turn to God and Rejoice in Hope." This 50th anniversary assembly reaffirmed the covenant made by the first assembly in Amsterdam (1948) by committing afresh to fellowship with one another by involving in concerns such as unity, justice, peace, and the integrity of creation in the context of globalisation.

Globalisation and its negative effects as well as natural calamities, terrorist acts and the war against terrorism, and scourges like drug trafficking formed the backdrop of the 2006 WCC assembly held in Porto Alegre, Brazil. At the heart of this assembly was a prayer, "God, in your grace, transform the world", which was partly a response to the slogan of the 2004 "World Social Forum" held in Brazil. This also reflected humankind's helplessness in his/her efforts to repair the damages that his/her greed and selfishness had caused to creation.

Porto Alegre recognised that churches, the agents of God's transformation of the world, are not exempted from globalisation and its negative effects. The assembly also noted that the constant influence of the media, managed by large transnational corporations, was creating alienation and consumerist illusions and frustrations among the young. The churches then articulated that the dependence on God should be seen in our trust in God's grace and move us to work for a better world. Porto Alegre also stressed on the transformation of the world in relation to the values of the kingdom of God.

ECC, as it was set up, was not for a monolithic form of unity of all mainline churches of India, but for the conciliar form of unity, as brought out by WCC's Uppsala assembly and given final shape at Nairobi.

5

Guiding Principles of ECC

There was a genuine attempt to translate the basic philosophy of the centre – wider ecumenism – into its concerns, awareness and action plans. The centre was true to its four basic thrusts – the unity of the churches (healing of the divisions in the body of Christ), the unity of faiths (search for a theological understanding of other faiths), the unity and renewal of humankind (discovery of authentic options for the healing of human brokenness), and the integrity of creation (maintaining a caring attitude towards all living beings).

*– **ECC:** Report of M.J. Joseph, director,*
Ecumenical Christian Center, 2001

Since the beginning of the ECC, it has been conducting seminars, training courses and national and international conferences. Besides, the ECC has been involving in community development and health services. All these activities reflect the programme dynamics of the ECC, as pointed out by former director M.J. Joseph above.

The centre has been giving adequate attention to the four thrusts mentioned above in its various programmes. The unity of churches, in the midst of divisions, was one of the main concerns of the ECC. Ecumenism, as traditionally understood, denoted the unity of all churches and mission societies under a common Christian umbrella. But this was just one part of the ecumenism concept that came to be articulated by experts.

However, in the course of the development of the ecumenical movement, the content of ecumenism was expanded to the whole of creation, irrespective of religion, race, caste or sex. We have already seen in the earlier chapters how this concept developed. ECC, in its programmes, imbibed this spirit of ecumenism and its activities did not confine to ecclesiastical unity alone, but to the unity of the whole creation.

It has reflected the four thrust areas, as mentioned above, in four different phases in the 44 years of its existence since 1963. Its directors – M.A. Thomas, Susy Nellithanam, K.C. Abraham, Mithra Augustine, M. J. Joseph and Mani Chacko – have worked hard to translate these thrusts into action plans during their tenures under the guidance of the board of directors and the executive committee.

COMMON PLATFORM FOR CHURCHES

The unity of churches has been an implicit emphasis of ECC, although it has not been expressed explicitly in its programmes and activities.

M. A. Thomas, in *'A Leap into the Unknown'*, says:

> *"From the beginning, it was my desire to develop it as a common platform of the Christian Churches in India."*

His plan for the initial years was for the centre to communicate Christ's message of love with a view to bring all churches in India together, although the concept of wider unity was always there on Thomas' radar screen. However, on 15[th]April, 1967, a special resolution was passed at the annual meeting of the governing council to delete sub clause (2) of the Memorandum of Association of the ECC because this clause gave the impression that the ECC's purpose was the unification of all Christian denominations. This showed ECC's seriousness to further the cause of wider ecumenism.

Nevertheless, in its first five years of existence, the centre's main emphasis was on church relations and unity. This emphasis was embedded in the conciliar unity model that was different from the earlier models of ecumenism, namely organic unity and spiritual unity. Organic unity connotes a merger of churches in their ecclesiastical and physical existence, while spiritual unity denotes a loose unity of churches, where all churches have common grounds for unity through the Holy Spirit. Every act of unity is a gift of the Holy Spirit, who binds churches together and enables them to give visible expressions to the desire of Jesus Christ for unity.

Conciliar fellowship may be defined as fellowship among churches that are already united through a common confession of faith, common participation in the Holy eucharist and mutual recognition of ministries. Conciliar fellowship – which is essentially a gathering together of churches to take decisions relating to church life, ministry and missions – is a necessary expression of the churches' organic oneness in Christ under the guidance of the Holy Spirit.

The baptism, eucharist and ministry document of the WCC in Lima, often referred to as the Lima document, is considered as the underlying agreement supporting the concept of conciliar fellowship. In India, this was given concrete shape for the first time by the Church of South India

(CSI), the Church of North India (CNI) and the Mar Thoma Church, which came together for a conciliar fellowship under the CSI, CNI, Mar Thoma Joint Council in 1977. It was renamed the Communion of Churches in India in 2000, institutionalising the concept with an office for the communion and the appointment of a secretary.

The concept of conciliar fellowship has been the emphasis of the World Council of Churches since the 1970s. ECC has been committed to the spread of this model of unity of all churches, advocating the conciliar approach as the appropriate model of ecclesiastical unity. Its programmes, since the 1970s, have been tailored to uphold this emphasis.

ECC has reflected this principle from its inception in 1963 by drawing its administrative and programme staff from different national churches. All mainline churches in India, including the Roman Catholic Church, have taken membership in the ECC. It's worth recalling here that the ECC building's architect was a Roman Catholic priest, Father J. M. Stevens.

"The Ecumenical Christian Centre is an institution truly ecumenical in character. Roman Catholics have also been involved in the work of the centre from the very inception in 1963, including providing members to our staff. At the moment, a Franciscan father is a member on our executive committee. We have three Roman Catholics in our programme staff. A leading industrialist from the Orthodox Church is our treasurer. All our programmes are held with the utmost emphasis on the involvement and participation of WCC-related churches and the Roman Catholic Church. This ecumenical character will be maintained in the regions that we plan to organize the schools on development issues."

*– **M. A. Thomas,** in a letter to Frere Christophe von Wachter, SODEPAX, Ecumenical Centre, Geneva*

As mentioned above, ECC was to establish schools on politics and economics in the later years. It also set up a National Citizens Academy, the Vicharodaya College and the Indian School of Ecumenical Theology. These will be explained in the following chapters.

The above letter by M.A. Thomas reflects ECC's central focus in the first phase of its existence, which was to bring all churches into a deeper union without losing their distinctiveness. ECC has been advocating for a unity in which various types of ecclesiastical bodies would exist side by side in local situations, fully recognising each other's ministry and institutional rites of baptism and the eucharist.

The ECC thus provided a platform for churches in India to discuss matters of common national and ecclesiastical interest. Churches of different denominational backgrounds find a common meeting place in ECC and this itself is a visible expression of the desire for unity of all churches.

The first phase of ECC's development, as obvious in the table below, focused on church-related programmes.

ECC's CHURCH-RELATED PROGRAMMES
IN THE FIRST PHASE

Year	No. of Programmes	Duration	Topic of the Programme
1963	3	1 day	ECC and Church Clergy
		1 day	ECC and Church Clergy
		8 days	Meeting friends of ECC's Christian Ministry

1964	4	1 day	Christian Responsibility
		3 days	Christian Participation in Journalism
		2 days	Christian Participation in Journalism
		1 day	Role of Laity/ Christian Family
1965	16	1 day	Church and its Challenges
		10 days	Christian Leadership Training

In the three years from 1966, ECC organised an average of two programmes a year in relation to the Church. The Church-related programmes can be classified under four heads, namely:

I.   Theological and ecumenical reflection

II. Responsibility of the Church in society

III. Focus on liturgy and worship

IV. Leadership training programmes

The centre has invited experts in theology and ecumenism to come together and reflect on their knowledge in the light of contemporary realities and has thus served as a place for theological and ecumenical learning. It believes that the Indian churches are catalysts for change along a secular and egalitarian line and has organised programmes to further this belief. The conferences at the ECC have been arranged in such a way as to educate the Indian churches on the social, political, cultural and economic realities of India.

It should be noted here that these programmes were offshoots of WCC's paradigm shifts in its understanding of unity, witness and mission after the 1950s. The moulding of responsible citizens also came to be understood as an ecclesiastical responsibility in the Indian context. M.A. Thomas understood these trends, imbibed them and translated them into practical reality.

He also sensed a need in the Indian post-Independence scenario for changes in worship patterns with a view to involve various denominations, faiths and communities for nation-building. His thinking was that leaders and youth in the Church could serve as a catalyst for change in this process.

ECC organises programmes and seminars every year to equip church leaders and the youth to formulate relevant worship patterns suiting the needs of the time. Besides, short-term study courses are also arranged by the centre at its "School of Worship" to enlighten the clergy and the laity.

ECC's programmes are usually not only held on its campus at Whitefield but also in other selected areas. For instance, "mobile programmes" were organised on ecumenical topics in places like Bellary in the Indian state of Karnataka, Vellore and Madras in Tamil Nadu and Guntur in Andhra Pradesh during 1964-67. Both Roman Catholics and Protestants participated in these programmes.

In an inclusive approach, ECC, through these programmes, was trying to empower the participants to hold an ecumenical vision and social responsibility.

"The Centre provides a certain Christian climate and atmosphere for all people. This in itself is a silent witness to the love of God revealed in Jesus Christ."

– M. A. Thomas: *Silent Witness*

UNITY OF FAITHS

In the second phase, ECC started emphasising the need to radiate the love of God, as revealed in Christ, to all mankind. This would manifest in common action and cooperation among peoples of different faiths and ideologies. This was a continuation of a theme that has been under development by the WCC since the 1961 New Delhi assembly. This theme was taken forward for discussions in Uppsala in 1968 and articulated, in clearer terms, in the 1983 Vancouver assembly document.

This new awareness of a world perspective of religious pluralism and the search for the possibilities of a greater measure of cooperation and understanding among different religious, cultural and ethnic communities was the basic vision underlining ECC's second phase. This vision has no hesitation in accepting the various socio-cultural roots of other religions or ideologies in a pluralistic society. It calls churches to take concerted efforts in understanding the mission of the world in relation to the values of God's kingdom. The concept encompasses all vulnerable communities, including the poor and women, and even all other living creatures.

Through the programmes in the second phase, ECC also started highlighting that the idea of ecumenism is context-based and is relevant to the multi-religious situation in India, the country of its existence.

It also tried to develop a community of concerned people to promote action for social change and to establish unity of humankind. M. A. Thomas believed that the mission of God in Christ was for the attainment of a new humanity for all mankind, as suggested in the report below:

> *Therefore, I decided that "… the Ecumenical Christian Centre had to feel the pulse of the nation and work in tune with it." In a country like India with its complexities and its struggles for a secular state, the ECC became conscious of its role for the furtherance of a secular and egalitarian society.*
>
> **ECC:** *The Report of the Executive Committee to the Governing Council, 14th June, 1969*

The table below shows how ECC manifested this vision in its programmes during 1970-'75.

PROGRAMMES ON THE SECULAR WORLD

S. No.	Year	No. of Programmes	Duration	Theme of the Conference
1)	1970	8	5wks each	Politics (5 programmes)
			1wk	Economics
			1wk	Efficacy of Administration
			1 day	Conference for Teenagers
2)	1971	6	1 day	Youth and Culture
			1 day	International Students Meet
			1wk	Teenagers Camp
			1wk	Personnel Management

			1wk	Education
			1wk	Changing Society
3)	1972	9	1wk	Changing Indian Society
			4mths	Inter-Religious Dialogue
			10 days	School of Sociology
			3 days	Press and People
			3 days	Judiciary and Parliament
			1 day	Youth and Drugs
			1wk	Teenagers
			1wk	Teenagers
			1wk	Personnel Management in Hospitals
4)	1974	10	1mth	Communalism in Indian Politics (3 programmes)
			3 days	Politics
			5 days	Federation in India
			3 days	Media and Politics
			1 day	Cinema and Social Change
			3 days	Harijan Oppression
			3 days	Education and Moral Values in Community

This phase saw the ECC's growing emphasis towards social, political, economic and inter-religious concerns. Most ECC programmes began to be organised keeping in view the ultimate goal of achieving unity of all humanity, addressing contemporary life situations. In this regard, it is worth recalling again the words of the founder:

> *"I was convinced that its style of functioning should be basically different from the familiar conservative style of churches. I came to the firm conclusion that the hallmark of the centre should be such activities as would bear witness to Christ meaningfully and hasten changes in the unjust social structure."*
>
>   **– M. A. Thomas,** *in a* letter *to Frere Christophe von Wachter, SODEPAX, Ecumenical Centre, Geneva*

ACTION IN RESPONSE TO SUPPRESSION

The 1975 "emergency" situation declared in India by former Prime Minister Indira Gandhi infringed on justice and human rights. This was perhaps the triggering point for the launch of ECC's third phase. During the late sixties and early seventies, there was enthusiasm and hope in the country for its democratic future, which were being dashed by one draconian act. This led to the ECC hoisting justice and human rights issues to the centrestage. Said former Bangalore Archbishop P. Arokiasamy, a former vice-chairman of the ECC:

> *ECC stands for justice and for human dignity. Wherever there is injustice, it will raise its voice against it – in India and elsewhere. That is the role it has set for itself.*
>
>   **– Arokiasamy:** *Speech at ECC's 20th Anniversary Celebrations on 14ᵗʰ March, 1983*

ECC strongly believes that the struggle for human rights is unending. History shows that freedom has to be fought for and liberty has to be won through battles. The founding of human rights action group Vigil India movement by the ECC in 1977, was a result of this strong belief.

Vigil India movement had its origins in ECC's School of Politics and Institute of Human Rights, which conducted courses during the emergency that provided an intense introduction to the Indian political system, structure and processes. It also tried to analyse specific political issues in India in the context of the "emergency" situation, especially the curtailment of the freedom of expression, as manifested in censorship decrees, suppression of political opponents and covert monitoring of people's movements. The result was the realisation of the need for action groups in the country as part of the centre's mission.

On 29th June, 1977, Vigil India movement was formally inaugurated, with M.A. Thomas as the founder director. The work of Thomas in the human rights realm had been noted even before the founding of Vigil India as he was the vice-president of the Indian chapter of global human rights watchdog Amnesty International. The Vigil India movement served to train leaders to form action groups in different parts of the country for monitoring the justice and human rights situation and giving voice to the voiceless. As a result, vigil groups were established in most Indian states.

ECC also gave importance to human values in the third phase. The institution believes that it has a role to play as a peacemaker or ambassador engaged in the ministry of reconciliation as part of a greater sense of purpose and expectation in the total life of the Indian nation.

Worth mentioning here is a novel initiative on the part of the centre in the Indian context. Since the second and third phases, it has been bringing together politicians of different hues under one roof to discuss contemporary political issues and concerns with a view to help form policies towards building a just, egalitarian and democratic nation.

INTEGRITY OF CREATION

The relationship of man with his surroundings has always been a special concern of ECC. A new emphasis on these issues was provided in the fourth phase.

Since 1984, seminars have been arranged at the center on environmental issues and concerns. However, a new emphasis was given to ecological concerns in ECC after 1997. The report of the director about the perspectives and programmes in 1997 says:

> *"Matters like the utilisation of physical resources for horticultural operations, setting up of social forestry, a garden on the western side of the campus, laying of a stone-laden footpath along the lake side, a herbal garden on the campus, a horticultural nursery, documentation of books and newspaper reports on environmental issues in India, academic treatment of ecological topics in the syllabus of the courses of ECC's Indian School of Ecumenical Theology (ISET), promoting justice concerns in ecology, publication of a brochure on the environmental concerns of ECC etc are some of the steps taken at the centre towards the realisation of the eco-vision of the centre."*

> **– M. J. Joseph, former director, ECC:**
> *Report of the Director*

The centre introduced planting of trees on special occasions and celebrations to actualise its eco-vision. The ECC set up a herbal garden on its campus with a view to encouraging alternative forms of medicine. Since one of the agendas of ecumenism is to work for the integrity of creation, the ECC has taken paramount care to include the same in its mode of functioning.

It is an acknowledged fact that any damage to the eco-system is against the principle of the affirmation of life. So caring for God's creation has become a guiding force for the mission of the Church in the 21st century. Environmental issues are discussed in almost all programmes of the centre. ECC celebrates festivals such as Christmas, Easter, Kannada New Year festival, Ugadi, and the Indian festival of lights, Deepavali, in a way that brings forth the message of caring for the environment. The centre has tried to ensure the participation of all communities in its neighbourhood in these programmes.

The resources of all people on earth have to be pooled together in seeking a God-given answer to the vexed problems of humanity today. Environmental management is essential in order to manage land, water and other natural resources for sustainable life on earth. ECC's special emphasis on environmental concerns has been serving as a wake-up call to participants in these programmes.

To sum up, ECC has indeed made a unique imprint in the ecumenical history of India by initiating programmes for educating the Indian people towards realising its emphasis on wider ecumenism. With its growth, the priorities of the centre have taken a new track, although it has never lost sight of its original objectives.

Its original emphasis had been the unity, harmony and rejuvenation of the churches. However, incorporating the unity of all human beings as well as ecological concerns in its goal has widened this emphasis. This shift has been the result of the positive response of the centre to the new initiatives of the WCC since 1961. Besides, ECC has served as a catalyst to motivate social action for the liberation of the Indian masses and to direct them towards a just, democratic and egalitarian society.

Though ECC is primarily a conference and study centre, it has provided a meeting place for people both in India and from abroad to discuss social, economic, political, and religious issues. It serves as a centre for unity of all human beings. At the same time, it responds to contemporary challenges both in the ecumenical and national realms.

6

Wider Ecumenism in Action

When the history of India comes to be written, this decade will find reference to the role of the Whitefield centre for the contribution it has made to the cause of democratic institutions and for the equipment of citizens to function as well-informed units. Indeed, our political system will be toned up and our parties will be disciplined by the emergence of this type of movement doing definite good to human beings.

– Eminent jurist V.R. Krishna Iyer:
Speech on the occasion of the 20ᵗʰ Anniversary of ECC

The ECC has been committed to the problems of the Indian society with a spirit of theological concern and the words above by Justice Krishna Iyer, an eminent jurist and champion of human rights and justice concerns, are an endorsement of this commitment. Millions in India are unaware of the real socio-political and cultural situation and ECC believed that unity is possible only when these vulnerable people became a uniting link in the socio, political and cultural development of the nation. Real unity is possible only through proper training and by equipping people to meet the needs of the nation.

It followed then that the country needed dynamic institutional expressions of wider unity. This was essential for the formation of a just, egalitarian and democratic system. In order to meet these needs, the ECC organised short-term and long-term courses in sociology, economics, politics, worship and so on. All these courses were aimed at bringing awareness about the problems of the Indian society to the participants. Besides, these helped to provide trained leaders to the nation for making changes in their respective areas.

The ECC has divided its programmes into eight sections, namely, seminars and conferences, training, Church-oriented programmes, community development, study projects to encourage participants in areas of social relevance, survey and research, and publications of books and regular periodicals. To accomplish its task it has full-time programme staff in various fields.

The ECC has been actively involved in various training programmes. Notable among these are the National Citizen's Academy, School of Politics, School of Economics, Vicharodaya College and Indian School of Ecumenical Theology (ISET).

A HELPING HAND TO NATION-BUILDING

The latter part of the sixties was replete with widespread optimism and enthusiasm to rebuild the nation. Responding to this challenge, the ECC started the National Citizenship Academy in 1968. This was an annual six-month postgraduate course for men. Graduates from all parts of India who attended this course were helped to widen their socio-political horizons with a view to help them lead in nation-building.

The main aim of the academy was to instill in the participants a consciousness for national service and to churn out a nucleus of intelligent, responsible and committed young men who would be agents of social change – men who would be ready to give their full co-operation and utilise their leadership abilities to usher in a new, secular and egalitarian society.

These young men were helped in their training with lectures, conferences, demonstrations and educational tours. The main purpose of this programme was to bring out a witnessing core group, the members of which would have had an experience of renewed life at the academy in the light of the love of God. They would then go out and spread this renewal experience all over the country.

This, it was envisaged, would help in transforming and renewing the whole nation.

The course curriculum made an attempt to train young men to study the social, economic and political forces at work in the various social, political and economic spheres. This would equip them in developing a perspective for a just and democratic nation bringing together all citizens.

The academy syllabus included programmes of political parties, the Indian constitution, rule of law, racial integration, *panchayati raj* (local self-government) five-year plans, land reforms, population problem, community development, mass communication and international affairs. After the completion of training, students would be equipped for a more meaningful involvement in nation-building wherever they were placed.

Selected students were placed in action projects and in programmes to monitor human rights situation. Some others involved themselves in politics and in economic and social planning programmes.

The students at the academy left with a sense of India's glorious past, but were awakened to the dark spots of the country's present. The academy moved them to be catalysts for social change.

Along the way, the academy evolved from its earlier nation-building perspective to be a school that would shape leaders to protect the cherished values of democracy. The turning point would come in 1971, when the political climate in the country changed for the worse with the declaration of emergency.

The emergency situation brought out a felt need for active cadres to protest against the erosion of democratic values in the country. The ECC started involving in a new style of operation from 1977 onwards through the Vigil India movement, which, as explained in the previous chapter, set up vigil groups across the country.

As the ECC started getting involved in Vigil India, which was actually an offshoot of the National Citizenship Academy, the centre started giving more emphasis was put on the movement, arguably at the cost of the academy. The academy had its last session in 1977.

COURSES AT NATIONAL CITIZENSHIP ACADEMY

	Year	Course duration	Participants	Focus of the Course
1	1968	6 months	18	Socio-political changes
2	1969	3 months	12	Politics and social change
3	1970	6 months	15	Politics and social change

The academy did make efforts to create awareness about the contemporary socio-political trends in India. It is a fact that young graduates of the 1970s were interested in participating in the six-month post-graduate course although this was not affiliated to any university.

The National Citizen's academy was a distinctive experiment in education. During this course, there was an earnest attempt to study the various forces at work in India which shaped the destiny of her people. Says A. S. Theodore, the first programme secretary of the National Citizens' academy:

> *The ECC aims at bringing men and women from various occupations with requisite educational background to come into fellowship not only with one another but also with the staff of the centre and the guest teachers. It would be a community in which the members bring with them fresh ideas, fresh problems, as well as fresh contributions from their own vivid experiences.*
>
> *They, in turn, can fertilize and enrich the entire programme as well as help them take back to their own environment, new insights relevant to the contemporary problems to share with their fellows. The hallmark of democracy is its inherent strength to create leadership. The Citizen's Academy could be one of the seedbeds for generating such leaders who have not only a vision but also the zeal to serve the nation – a new breed of missionaries – that India needs today.*
>
> **– A.S. Theodore:**
> *Report of the Programme Secretary,*
> *National Citizens' Academy, 1968*

However, it is a fact that many of the young men and women who participated in the course could not involve themselves in social action due to the various circumstantial pressures and M. A. Thomas himself admitted as much. These pressures include the caste system prevalent in the country, financial constraints, lack of universal education and the general apathy of the middle class society, from which most of the participants hailed from, towards social problems.

M. A. Thomas says:

They are participating in socio-political activities and have fared well. They are exceptions. It is easy to train young people who come from middle class homes to involve in radical movements for social change, but it is difficult for them to do anything radical because of social and financial constraints. Yet what these courses were able to offer was a plus point to their lives. It helped them to look beyond themselves and to have some concern for others.

– **M. A. Thomas:** *A Leap Into The Unknown*

One of the positive results of the academy was that it acted as an educational agency for young graduates in bringing awareness about the socio-political system of India. The emphasis of the programme was to produce competent leaders, who would help promote greater involvement of the people. However, the academy's contribution to the society was neither spectacular nor radical.

Still, the formation of the Vigil India movement in 1977 and the organization of 'vigil groups' in different Indian states by academy graduates were visible offshoots of the academy. Having formed 'vigil groups' in different places, proper training was given to the young participants. M. A. Thomas says "vigil groups were born from these courses in various areas". This helped the centre to pool together a group of people for a national cause.

SCHOOL OF ECONOMICS

The ECC started a 'School of Economics', a ten-day residential course, in 1968. Students from all over India came to the centre every year to attend the course. It provided opportunities and experience to participants through lectures and discussions and tried to enable them to reflect on the problems common to the Indian citizens in the socio-economic and political realms.

The course aimed at highlighting the importance of political ideology in accelerating economic and social development in India, besides in making the youth the agents of social change. ECC believed that the entire educational system of the country must undergo radical change and the school of economics was an experiment in this direction. Among the other objectives of the school were the development of the nation and the assessment of the current economic trends in the country.

Issues like nationalism, unemployment, under-development, property rights, models for India's growth, foreign aid, labour, privy purse and Indian economy and green revolution were studied in the light of their social, political and cultural implications. Resource persons from political parties presented their economic policies and struggles for achieving social justice. Other resource persons included leading economists and economics teachers like Prof. M. A. Oommen and Dr C. T. Kurien.

The school of economics has played the role of a conscientiser by introducing the Indian economic and political system to the participants. It is an acknowledged fact that the 1960s was a turbulent period in India's political economy. Though the five-year plans commenced in 1961, the Chinese aggression and the Pakistani war adversely affected the implementation of the plan.

Political parties like the Congress (Socialist), Jan Sangh, Communist Party of India (CPI), and the Communist Party of India – Marxist (CPI-M) actively sent their cadres to the School of Economics.

The food problem in the early sixties, and the subsequent foreign exchange crisis prompted the government to approach multinational companies for help. The nationalisation of 14 big private banks by former Prime Minister Indira Gandhi was a major economic policy initiative during those years. The School of Economics has provided a platform to the participants to discuss these developments in India and to equip themselves in becoming responsible citizens of India.

SCHOOL OF POLITICS

A one-month residential course was offered by ECC in 1968 with a view to providing an intense introduction to the Indian political systems, structures and processes, as well as independent analyses of specific political issues.

M.A. Thomas says:

"Our emphasis is not on academic understanding but on a contemporary analysis of the socio-economic and political dynamics with a pointer towards the urgent need for commitment to action."

   – **M. A. Thomas:** *Interview with P.D. Devadasan*

Delegates from all over India have participated in this course, which aims to provide participants with an awareness of the factors needed for a just, democratic and egalitarian political system. It gives an opportunity for those interested in politics to critically study the policies and programmes of the various political parties in India, the current political and economic trends and the various aspects of the Indian constitution.

A variety of subjects has been included in the curriculum of the school of politics. These include political ideologies, Indian political systems, masters of political thought, the Constitution of India, theoretical aspects of politics and parliamentary democracy. According to Sucy Nellithanam:

> *The mood of the nation during the emergency (1975-'77) and after convinced the centre that radical words should be explained through radical action. The major part of 1977 was devoted to giving political training to young men and women by conducting courses of a two-week duration. Around 350 young people were trained during this period besides the usual conference and consultation.*

– **Sucy Nellithanam:** *Ripples –*
Story of the Ecumenical Christian Centre,
1960-1980

During the Indian emergency, the school served to inspire a number of participants to work against the draconian regime. It called for radical action to preserve democracy. In order to achieve this and as a follow-up to the centre's involvement in conscientising political cadres during the emergency, an intensive training programme was started at the centre in 1977.

Simultaneously, the centre started mobile training programmes of the School of Politics in Bellary in Karnataka state, Guntur in Andhra Pradesh and in parts of Tamil Nadu, Kerala and some other states with a view to impart objective training to more young men and women on Indian politics. Among the variety of subjects discussed were the necessity of politics, philosophy of Gandhi, and current economic trends, democracy and non-violence, relevance of Gandhiji for the present age, nationalism versus regionalism and propaganda methods of political parties. Besides, special study programmes were organised occasionally at the centre to discuss the socio-political issues in India.

PROGRAMMES OF THE SCHOOL OF POLITICS

Serial No	Year	Course Duration	Number of Participants	Focus of the Programme
1)	1984	3 months	14	Politics and social change
2)	1984	10 days	129	Politics and social change
3)	1987	3 months	11	Politics and social change
4)	1991	21 days	29	Political systems
5)	2001	10 days	18	Socio-political development
6)	2002	10 days	19	Communalism in India
7)	2004	7 days	28	Secularism in India

The duration of the courses offered by the school of politics was thus reduced from three months to seven days over 20 years. At the same time, the number of participants did not increase considerably. What had happened, as interviews with staff and former directors at the ECC showed, was a steady decline in interest among the youngsters on political issues. It must be said here that the centre was not able to draw to the school enough youngsters who would be deeply committed to issues of common interest and politics.

Meanwhile, the socio-political shift that happened in the country after the demolition of the Babri Masjid on 6th December, 1992, by Hindu fanatics and the subsequent politicisation of religion compelled ECC to train youth on the growing threat of communalism. This is apparent in the changing focus, as shown in the table, of the school programmes from political to socio-political and religious issues.

The school of politics has imparted political awareness to groups of young people on the Indian political situation and inspired them to fight for the marginalised and oppressed. For instance, the School disregarded the emergency rules, and participants were encouraged to express their views openly about the emergency. And many did come out sharply against emergency and the then Prime Minister, Indira Gandhi. M.A. Thomas assured the participants that they were free to air their views, when Michael Fernandes, a political leader and a speaker at a school of politics conference during the emergency, enquired about this.

The school has helped bring to focus the struggles and aspirations of the suffering people in our country, particularly the struggle for justice, human rights, dignity and social justice. For example, Snehalatha Reddy, a friend of the ECC worked for human rights during the emergency period and was arrested and subjected to inhuman torture in prison. She died within a few days of her release. The poor continue to be shattered by vested interests, but the school of politics helps to conscientise them towards putting their hopes in politics. The centre has been in the search of a new kind of politics that ensures more participation of people.

Some participants conscientised by the school of politics have found their vocation in furthering the cause of human rights. Among them is Mathews George Chunakkara, who went on to be an executive secretary of the Vigil India movement, which was founded by the ECC to fight for the protection of human rights, and is now the present executive secretary of the WCC's Asia desk.

Apart from these, the school's programmes have introduced participants to life skills that equip them to react constructively and creatively to social and political situations as well as to assess the needs of the society and forge ways of responding to them. The programmes have been geared to enable alert, analytical and critical reactions to life situations. This in turn has helped in creating political and socially responsible citizens at the grassroots level.

Their efforts have resulted in bringing together people belonging to different faiths and ideologies for a just society, providing added meaning to the concept of wider ecumenism.

VICHARODAYA COLLEGE

Vicharodaya College is a women's college for dynamic education. It was formally inaugurated in ECC by the late Yuhanon Mar Thoma Metropolitan on June 15, 1972. Vicharodaya means the "dawn of knowledge."

> *"Vicharodaya was a programme that the Ecumenical Christian Centre conducted annually to train young women graduates for a period of six months or one year to instil in them a consciousness for national service."*
>
> **– M.A. Thomas:** *A Leap Into The Unknown*

The college was started with a view to creating social concern among young women in India. The basic principle behind starting the college was to help release the frozen talent of the educated woman for the service of the wider community and to run a better home.

The training institution served mainly to mould women into responsible and self-reliant citizens in a male-dominated social system. It aimed at empowering women to become resourceful as wives, colleagues, mothers and as dynamic catalysts in the welfare of the society.

The curriculum of the college was planned to include various subjects under four heads; namely, individual and family, individual and society, art and culture and India and the wider world. The exposure participants got through the course would help them face the challenges of life.

Apart from topics such as family, social ties, and economic development, Vicharodaya participants discussed various women-related issues in rural and urban settings and also the role of educated women in the community and in public bodies.

The programme also focused on the stereotypical image of Indian women as portrayed in arts and culture. The portrayal of women in literature, cinema, paintings, sculpture, advertising and theatre were examined critically. In most Indian art forms, women have been depicted as docile, chaste and helpless and have always been seen in relation to male counterpart and never as intelligent individuals by their own right. Apart from the classroom exposure, Vicharodaya students visited nearby villages of the centre and a lively relationship was established with the villagers over the years. The students were also involved in the Balavadis run by the centre.

All these programmes helped to give the participants a wide exposure to social realities.

PROGRAMMES OF THE VICHARODAYA COLLEGE

No.	Year	Duration of the Course	Number of Participants	Focus of the Course Year
1)	1972	1 year	20	Social Concerns and Development
2)	1973	1 year	18	Personal Development and Social Concerns
3)	1980	6 months	14	Cry for Justice in our Midst
4)	1985	3 months	13	Education & Social Change
5)	1988	3 months	12	Education for Liberation
6)	1990	1 month	5	Contemporary Social Concerns

As revealed in the table above, there had been a decline in the number of participants from 1972, when the programme was, to 1998, when the Vicharodaya College was stopped. The duration of the course was also reduced from one year in 1972 to just about a month by 1990 and up to 1998. The reasons offered by the ECC for this situation are two-fold. The first was the practical difficulty in getting young women graduates to spend long periods at the college for socially-relevant courses, when there were other vocational courses available in mainstream educational institutions. Moreover, the ECC felt that it was more meaningful in training larger numbers of young women in short-duration courses rather than bringing in small groups for year-long, six-month and three-month courses.

From 1998 onwards, the course was reduced to a week's programme on women's rights. The poor attendance of candidates in the one-year programme, non-affiliation of the course to any mainstream university degree, the centre's change of emphasis from social realities to a more focused theme of women's rights, and lack of funds were some of the reasons for the decline of the Vicharodaya initiative.

The course created consciousness among the participants on the violations of human rights of women and weaker sections of the society in workplaces and in other situations, besides the need for women to be involved in national service. However, it was reported that not all graduates of Vicharodaya had taken to social service, although a considerable number of them had identified themselves with movements for positive action after gaining new insights from the centre.

M.A. Thomas used to say:

"These courses are meant to give women a plus point wherever they are so that they may cease to be inward looking but looking beyond with a concern for others."

– **M. Kurien:** *A Quest for the Unknown*

The ECC believed that development and cultural revolution would be a remote possibility without the active participation of the women and the vulnerable communities in India.

Socio-economic and political subjects were also discussed in this course, exposing students to a world dominated by suffering and injustice and helping them to realise that in a country like India, there was a struggle for economic and social justice that was needed prior to the emancipation of women.

It is a fact that the ECC has created a consciousness through these training courses, although without any commendable outcomes. The major reason for the not-so-great results, as M. A. Thomas was to note later, was the social and financial constraints of the participants. Graduates of Vicharodaya were to find on their return that their home situation was not yet conducive to put in practice what they learned.

Nevertheless, the ECC has helped impart knowledge about the Indian situation to the participants at the micro level in the hope that this would one day indirectly be manifested at the local and national level.

INDIAN SCHOOL OF ECUMENICAL THEOLOGY (ISET)

The 1975 WCC assembly held in Nairobi reiterated the need to mobilise a wider community of faiths to protect the harmony and rhythm in God's creation. The assembly, in its statement, emphasised the role of conciliar fellowship of all religious communities for the building up of a just society. Responding to this call, ECC's executive committee in 1976 proposed a school of ecumenical theology with a view to provide a platform for students and practitioners of theology to spread the message of wider ecumenism. In the context of the Indian emergency, the centre felt that a conciliar form of fellowship is essential to safeguard freedom, democracy and human rights in the nation. To achieve the goal of wider ecumenism, the centre and M. A. Thomas felt that a proper theological training institute rooted in the Indian context was essential.

"M. A. Thomas was deeply convinced about the necessity for a residential Indian School of Ecumenical Theology to help widen the ecumenical understanding and vision of theological teachers, clergy, youth and others, and through them, the church at large.

The general objective would be to support and supplement the basic philosophy of ECC – wider ecumenism."

– M. Kurien: *"A Quest for the Unknown"*

The ECC felt that theological seminaries, as learning grounds for church leaders, had a great role in bringing freedom and harmony among people of different faiths and communities in specific Indian urban and rural situations. Thomas envisaged ecumenism in ever-widening circles – "inter-church, inter-religious and cosmic – which together constitute the total ecumenical process".

The ECC executive committee resolved to take necessary steps to run the Indian School of Ecumenical Theology (ISET) – mainly for theological teachers – for an experimental period of three years. However, the involvement of ECC in other activities delayed the fruition of this proposal by about 12 years. ISET was established in 1988 and its first programme was a three-month course for teachers from theological colleges.

The school aims to create an ecumenical vision that involves three major thrusts - the Church, inter-religious dialogue and wider ecumenism. It also aims at creating a common commitment by all faiths and communities towards the building up of the kingdom of God. In effect, this helps to form a community of communities, which identifies with the sufferings of people and guides them towards social amity.

The objectives of ISET reflect ECC's vision of a wider ecumenism – the unity of all humankind. Its statement of objectives clearly expresses ISET's intentions:

- To take the total reality of the world, especially the Indian reality as the text and content of theologizing.

- To take account of the inter-church, inter-religious, socio-cultural and politico-economic reality of Asia and of the contemporary world.

- To involve all churches and wider human community in the process of theologizing so that theology becomes truly ecumenical.

- To discover and promote the rich diversity and the invaluable heritage of all Christian traditions and thus to contribute towards mutual understanding and enrichment.

- To promote dialogue and cooperation among living religious traditions, taking the Indian situation of religious pluralism as a gift and a task and working to evolve on a theology of religions.

- To foster the unity of all humankind and that of the entire creation by analysing the diverse and destructive forces at work in the world, exposing their root causes and proposing a way of healing and reconciliation and thus promoting peace with justice.

ISET exists mainly for teachers of theology, secular teachers, pastors and church leaders to help them see the purpose of God who has created a world of multiple living beings, races, cultures and religions. Its specific ministry is to help all Church denominations realise that they ought to follow the principle of unity and not of division.

ISET started with four major courses a year a one month courses for pastors, teachers in secular education, and for youth leaders and a three-month course for theological teachers. In addition to these residential programmes, regional institutes have been organized under the initiatives of ISET in Madurai and some other places in India. Research scholarship has been given to selected doctoral research scholars at the Dharmaram Vidyaksetra, Bangalore.

PROGRAMMES OF INDIAN INSTITUTE OF ECUMENICAL THEOLOGY

No	Year	Duration (months)	No of Courses for Pastors	Courses for Youth Leaders	Courses for Secular Teachers	Courses for Theology Teachers	Courses for Theology Students
1)	1988	1	16	–	–	–	–
2)	1989	1	25	20	22	6	–
3)	1990	1	33	20	23	8	–
4)	1991	1	21	43	19	68	–
5)	1992	1	25	26	13	15	86
6)	1993	1	20	25	21	12	94
5)	1994	1	28	26	15	10	99
6)	1995	1	16	34	14	19	68
7)	1996	1	19	13	32	26	64

ISET, with its various programmes for different categories of participants, such as pastors, youth leaders, secular teachers, theological teachers and students, has tried to bring together people of different faiths and ideologies to forge new relationships, to build bridges of understanding and collaboration in a world that is prone to fragmentation and divisions.

ISET has been publishing a journal, *"Theology for Our Times"* from 1994 onwards. This contains theological articles and common issues that India and the world are facing today. The articles discuss the various areas of our micro and macro level existence in the light of the need to foster the unity of humankind as well as the entire creation. The journal serves to make its readers aware of the realities in the contemporary world and focuses on areas that could form part of wider unity.

The courses in the ISET programmes have been developed keeping in focus ECC's wider ecumenism agenda. The realities of the contemporary situation are analyzed and evaluated. It is an acknowledged fact that an ecumenical theology can be developed only by seriously taking into consideration other faiths and secular ideologies. The ECC has developed this course as a forum to enter into a dialogue with different living faiths.

The members from other faiths – particularly from Hinduism, Islam, Sikhism, Buddhism, and Zoroastrianism – come together at the ISET courses. The participants from different religious backgrounds meet together and discuss diverse areas of national importance. Ecological concerns are also discussed in the ISET programmes.

INSTITUTE ON HUMAN RIGHTS

ECC has been organising an Institute on Human Rights every year since 1977 and a good number of participants have been those from non-governmental and organisations and churches. According to M. A. Thomas, "the struggle for human rights is unending. History shows that freedom has to be fought for and liberty has to be won through battles". Since the struggles for human rights are unending, the ECC felt it has to explore areas where human rights are violated in India. The Institute on Human Rights was established in the centre with this intention.

During the Emergency in March 1977, the ECC organised a one-month course on the theme 'vigilance' and various issues facing the country were discussed. In this meeting, the preliminary decision to form the Vigil India movement for resistance was taken. From 1998, the ECC divided the Institute on Human Rights into three institutes – the Institute on Women's Rights, Institute of Dalit and Tribal Concerns and Institute on Environmental Concerns.

INSTITUTE ON WOMEN'S RIGHTS

The Institute on Women's Rights has been organised by the Centre with a view to examine the instruments of social transformation, analyse the role of women as described by religious texts and traditions and to narrate stories of oppression of women in the society with a view to breaking the conspiracy of silence.

The Institute began work in 1998 with the aim to empower women's spiritually. In a situation where women's rights were trampled on, the Institute sought to invest in women participants from all over India an awareness of the existence of legal rights for their protection. Gender discrimination, displacement of tribals particularly women, and violence against women are realities in India.

PROGRAMMES OF THE INSTITUTE ON WOMEN'S RIGHTS

Year	Duration of Course	Number of Participants	Focus of the Course
1999	7 days	15	Gender Justice and Social Transformation
2000	7 days	29	Empowering of Women

Year	Duration of course	Number of participants	Focus of the course
2001	7 days	25	Empowering of Women
2002	4 days		Female foeticide: Women and HIV/ AIDS
2003	4 days		Empowering Women
2004	3 days	27	Women and Development

The ECC has incorporated women's issues in the category of human rights issues and it has given adequate attention to train women about contemporary issues of women in the society. Women from almost all Indian states have participated in its programmes and they have come from different cultural and religious backgrounds. The Institute of Women's Rights has been yet another avenue by which the ECC widened the horizon of ecumenism by including all susceptible groups in its agenda of activities.

INSTITUTE ON DALIT AND TRIBAL ISSUES

The centre has organised an Institute on Dalit and Tribal Issues every year since 2000. These issues have been often highlighted and are sensitive, but have still been ignored by the society. The ECC has drawn participants from various agencies in this training course that is aimed at imparting a wider understanding and knowledge about the present situation of dalits and tribals in India, as well as to strengthen their local struggles.

DETAILS OF THE INSTITUTE ON DALIT AND TRIBAL ISSUES

Year	Duration	Participants	Focus of the Programme
2000	8 days	24	Wider understanding of Dalit and Tribal Community
2001	8 days	21	Casteism and Human Rights in India
2002	8 days	23	Oppression of Dalit Women, Children, Caste and Class
2003	3 days	22	Dalit and Tribals Affirming Identities
2004	7 days	32	Dalit and Tribal Concerns

Since 2000, ECC has been giving some emphasis on dalits and tribal issues in Indian society. The centre is thus extending its agenda of wider unity by incorporating basic communities and their problems.

The institute has been able to bring together almost all major groups engaged in the struggles of the dalit and tribal communities on one platform and to help them create a network of action and a strategy to take their struggles forward. The ECC has thus been serving as an unifying agency for the cause of the struggles of India's vulnerable communities, which is no doubt a positive response to the need for wider unity in India.

INSTITUTE ON ENVIRONMENTAL CONCERNS

Since 1987, issues relating to justice, peace and integrity of creation have been the centre's main concerns. Ecological concerns also started receiving attention at the centre from

1992. The ECC felt the need for creating awareness for protecting the environment. This resulted in the formation of an Institute on Environmental Concerns in ECC in May 2000.

Institue participants are drawn from senior professionals, social activists, teachers, youths and missionaries. The centre has tried to incorporate a wide range of participants to study and act upon these issues.

**PROGRAMMES OF THE INSTITUTE ON
ENVIRONMENTAL CONCERNS**

Year	Duration of Course	Number of Participants	Programme Focus
2000	7 Days	22	Ecological Issues-Analysis of the problem
2001	7 Days	30	Ecological Issues-Analysis of the problem
2002	7 Days	27	Ecological Issues-Analysis of the problem
2003	3 Days	22	Ecological Issues-Analysis of the problem

The centre has incorporated the new dimension of ecological concerns into its wider unity focus and the Institute of Enviromental Concerns helps to explore the reasons for the environmental issues of human beings facing the world. The global community is facing an alarming situation as a result of the egocentric attitude of human beings. The participants at the institute pledge to work for the protection of the ecosystem. Through this initiative, the ECC has been trying to educate a section of the society about an alarming issue that man has been facing.

SPECIAL STUDY PROJECTS

The ECC has been arranging special study projects to encourage writers on topics of social change. The report of the annual general meeting of 1998 says:

> *"A series of 10 creativity weekends were organised for college students from Bangalore between November-December 1987. Creativity and creative expression belong to everyone, and everyone has the capacity to be creative. Poetry writing, painting, clay work, batik prints and street theatre were some of the areas focused on during these workshops."*

These study projects, including a one-month journalism course, were designed to equip participants with the skills in their areas of interest and to enable them understand critically the role of these creative expressions, especially in the struggles of the voiceless people of India, which constitutes the majority.

SURVEY AND RESEARCH

In order to gain a better understanding of the villages and their conditions, the centre conducts surveys of the physical infrastructure and health conditions of people in the villages of Karnataka and Tamil Nadu states. A survey of the conditions of the disabled was made in 1980, covering 12 villages in the Bangalore South Taluk situated around Whitefield. After the survey, 53 orthopaedically handicapped children, 15 blind children, some mentally retarted children and deaf and dumb children were referred to hospitals in Bangalore for treatment. These surveys and research throw light on the real picture of Indian villages, which is one of poverty, malnutrition, diseases and others socio-economic backwardness.

COMMUNITY DEVELOPMENT

One of the main objectives of ECC, as enshrined in its Memorandum of Association, is to provide socio-economic and medical relief to the poor and medical relief for the poor in India, irrespective of caste, creed or religion. The three components of the centre's community development programme – health, education and economic upliftment – aim at helping villagers in their overall growth and development.

The centre's community development programme concentrates on major areas of primary health, education for literacy, basic skills and social awareness. The economic programmes aim at better utilisation of resources, self-employment and self-help. The focus of the ECC in its community development programmes is the people as is evident in its programmes detailed below.

Balawadis: ECC organises its rural development activities by founding *balawadis* – day-care and primary education centre for poor children – in its neighbouring villages and also in some areas of Tamil Nadu and Andhra Pradesh. In 1980, the centre had 55 balawadis in Karnataka and 44 in Kanyakumari district in Tamil Nadu. Each *balawadi* has an average of 30 children. The Government of Karnataka has recognised ECC's *balawadis,* which undertake regular medical check-ups and immunization programmes for the children.

Health Programmes: Clinics have been established in neighbouring villages to look after the health of villagers. Besides, the centre conducted training programmes for medical personnel every year for encouraging them to do village work. A 20-day course on community health has been organised at the centre to train young men and women involved in health education to develop a holistic approach to health problems.

The centre has village clinics at Agrahara, Gandhipuram, Nallurhalli and the ECC campus in Bangalore. However, this ministry of ECC is not too active today.

Rural Development Projects: The rural development projects, started in 1980, are aimed at the holistic development of the villages. This area of work includes education, health and development of vulnerable people like the handicapped, blind, deaf etc. According to the report of the director for 1981-82:

> *We have extended our work to another village, Gandhipuram. Now in three villages, balawadis, clinics and other programmes are being carried out. A special stress of the programme has been on the rehabilitation of the handicapped. Steps are taken to assess the needs and to make the community aware of the needs for rehabilitating the disabled.*
>
> *– ECC: Director's Report presented to the annual general body meeting held on 19th June, 1982.*

Thus by 1982, ECC had taken initiatives for the rehabilitation of vulnerable communities. Frequent health surveys were arranged by the centre in nearby villages to identify sick villagers and to give them proper treatment. These surveys were held with the help of government hospitals in Bangalore.

The ECC has responded to people affected by natural calamities also. When a cyclone in 1973 completely destroyed some villages in Andhra Pradesh state, ECC adopted a village called Hyderpet and rehabilitated displaced villagers, on requests from friends in the state.

Community development activities of ECC today: The intensity of the centre's development works has diminished over time. However, ECC has continued its efforts for the empowerment of the community in its neighbourhood. Besides the balawadis, which are in service in three villages, an "Ecumenical Neighbourhood Empowerment Programme" (ENEP) was inaugurated in 2005 to strengthen the centre's relationship with the villagers. Care for the aged, water management, HIV/AIDS education classes, classes on environment, financial management and other training programmes have been conducted at the centre for the welfare of the community.

The empowerment of women has been a major agenda of ECC. It is committed to "women's rights" and has been acting as a catalyst for building up an inclusive society of love and peace. Together with Vicharodaya College, the centre has been involved in equipping young women to look at society in a different perspective. It equips women for meaningful living and helps them face the challenges in a community that has been dominated by caste system and male chauvinism. It also helps women to be harbingers of peace and justice by providing non-violent alternatives to overcome injustice. Special conferences are being arranged for both slum and urban women to discuss the socio-political situation of India.

ECC PUBLICATIONS

ECC has a publication wing that has so far published 15 books in English and one in Malayalam. A newsletter, *ECC News*, is published periodically. The centre also beings out occasional publication on contemporary issues. In addition to these, ISET has been publishing a journal namely, *Theology for Our Times*.

From 1993 onwards, lectures on contemporary issues delivered by renowned personalities during the annual M. A. Thomas Memorial Lectures are being published every year. These publications have been serving to educate people towards wider unity of all human kind.

ACISCA: The ECC has played a major role in forming an Association of Christian Institutes for Social Concerns in Asia (ACISCA) to link up centres that have similar concerns for the dispossessed and involved in nation building. It must be said here that ECC is the fourth largest centre of its kind in the world as far as its facilities and assets and programmes are concerned.

ECC stands for the promotion of wider unity at various levels in the life of the Church and nation. During the past 44 years, the centre has kept alive this vision and has carried on activities, particularly training programmes, for furthering ecumenical understanding and co-operation.

Among the channels to communicate the message of wider unity to different walks of people, the centre's long-term and short-term study courses has played a significant role.

However, there has been a steady decline in the long-term study courses. The participants no longer find any attraction in long-term courses. Furthermore, the involvement in social action has declined over the years. However, ECC has been continuing its mission to educate people belonging to all sections of society by conducting short-term seminars and training programmes.

Apart from this, a number of national and international guest conferences have been held on the campus on various subjects. These programmes have been a response of ECC to contemporary trends in the national and ecumenical scenarios. As a conscientiser, the ECC has been trying to communicate current trends and issues to the public through the participants of its various courses and through their common statements and ECC publications. However, it is doubtful whether participants have been able to spread the message to the targeted community in which they live in the same spirit as the centre has envisaged.

The centre has been introducing new study programmes regularly, but there is criticism that it has not been able to sustain its old programmes with the same vigour in which they were initiated. Nevertheless, there is an under-girding spirit of wider unity in the entire programme dynamics of the ECC.

In its four phases of activities, which have been described in an earlier chapter, the ECC has been able to communicate its emphasis of wider unity clearly through the training programmes and seminars. An analysis of the history of the ECC testifies to this fact.

In addition, the centre has been doing great service to the society in moulding public opinion through its training activities for a secular, democratic and egalitarian society in India. The idea has been to indirectly communicate the message that all Indians are brothers and sisters and the country cannot afford discord in the matter of religion, caste or language.

7

An ECC Balancesheet

The centre's function as a laboratory, which it has been till now, should continue. At any cost, it should not be lessened because this is one of the rarest laboratories we can see in the whole of India in which people of all faiths, all beliefs – even if they can't talk to each other or look at each others' face elsewhere – can come together and feel as a community. This is because of the thrusts of the founder and the administrators from the beginning that ECC's basic commitment is to humanity at large – not to one sect or one religion. That particular philosophical concept – the philosophy of the laboratory – must be maintained at any cost.

– **E. P. Menon:** *Speech on the occasion of ECC's 20th Anniversary*

It is an acknowledged fact that ECC is a product of the Indian ecumenical movement, and not a result of any Church movement. Its efforts towards fostering wider unity in the country have already been documented in the previous chapters. ECC was concerned about inter-church relations, but also occupying centrestage in its priorities was helping a fledgling country to grapple with issues of nation-building after the British imperialists left India in 1947. The foremost among its agenda has been to strive for a secular, democratic and inclusive society.

When we discuss the contributions of ECC, it should be noted that the centre has been responding to the shifts of emphasis in the world ecumenical realm, particularly to the paradigm shifts in the life and work of the WCC. Besides, it affirms the fact that ecumenism is essentially a cosmic vision primarily concerned with the discernment of the uniting presence of God in the world.

LABORATORY FOR WIDER ECUMENISM

In its 44 years of existence, the ECC has been recognised as an important ecumenical institution of international repute. In its popular sense, ecumenism promotes inter-church understanding and co-operation among different Christian denominations. But the broadening awareness of the world perspective of religious pluralism seeks a greater measure of co-operation and an expanding scope for ecumenism. This has opened a new style of functioning in the ecumenical movement that encompasses the whole of humankind. ECC has been striving all these years to incorporate these two emphases of ecumenical movement in its life and activities.

As we have seen, the great vision of M. A. Thomas was not merely Church unity, but the unity of all Indian citizens in order to bring a secular and democratic nation in India, on the one hand, and to achieve unity and co-operation among churches in India, on the other. That vision of ecumenism encompassed all Indians, irrespective of caste, creed and sex.

The centre found that an ecumenical perspective more suited to the country was one which could take into consideration the pluralistic context of the country. Hence, the originators of the ECC fashioned its goals towards working as agents of ecclesiastical unity and the unity of humanity as a whole. At the same time, ECC has always been sensitive towards the challenges of the time – particularly the challenges raised by the WCC from time to time and this has been described in Chapter IV.

PROMOTION OF SECULAR AND 'KINGDOM' VALUES

The four pillars of ECC's ecumenism philosophy have been described in Chapter V. These are the unity of churches, unity of other faiths, unity and renewal of mankind and the integrity of creation.

ECC has been striving to promote secular and spiritual values in inter-faith relations and in the study of ecology, science and religion, and remaining rooted in this ecumenical perspective has helped the centre go beyond a peripheral unity of churches and other faiths.

The ECC has been trying its best to keep a harmony of ideas and relationships. When churches come together under the ECC umbrella, there's an underlying harmony of the basic tenets of peace, justice, reconciliation and the hope of creation that is the realisation of God's kingdom. There is already a harmony of ideas there. At the same time, these are values cherished by all religions. Harmony of relationships in terms of living together and mutual respect is less fraught with tension and more achievable. Harmony of relationships should be spontaneous and natural.

However, the centre strongly believes that harmony and dialogue are not enough. A common ethos, a common society and a common spirit of nationhood are needed. Misconceptions about religions abound and ECC addressed this issue by introducing study sessions on various faiths.

The ministry of ECC during the last four decades has been based on the above-mentioned perspectives for the global community.

> *The challenge is in remembering and re-enacting the covenant – the unity of humankind. The role ECC has played in the last 25 years is to establish the covenantal relationship in a humble way between "myself and all that lives on earth." We will continue to affirm life in the coming years.*
>
> **– ECC:** *Report of the Annual General Body Meeting, 1988*

The relationship mentioned here is a reference to the covenant between God and man and the rest of the creation. All programmes of the centre in the last four decades have been geared to strengthen the covenant. The ECC has been able to harness the wider and deeper concerns of theologians and leaders of both the secular and the religious realms towards strengthening this covenant.

STRATEGY OF ECC

ECC has developed its own strategy to communicate ecumenical perspectives of wider unity to the people. This has been fashioned with a view to cover all cross-sections of Indian society. This strategy has manifested in mainly six ways as described below:

ECC has been conducting short-term and long-term training programmes both for the clergy, common people, intellectuals, women etc. The intention has been to enable the Church and society to have a trained cadre of people committed to the cause of secularism, social amity, peace, justice and environmental consciousness. These cadres would then make ripples in their respective areas, which would eventually be instrumental in fostering wider unity and the welfare of the nation.

Secondly, the ECC has been providing a platform to conduct seminars and conferences to groups that included social activists, ecumenists and inter-faith groups and non-government organisations. At the campus, these groups take in ECC's perspective of wider unity as reflected in its style of functioning – from the administrative block to the dining hall. This author was impressed by the fact that all staff of the centre – from the director to the cleaner – was treated equally at the workplace and the dining hall.

The centre's eco-friendly atmosphere conveys instructive as well as illustrative universal messages on the environmental dimension of wider unity to the visitors. The way the whole campus has been laid out provides insight into the need for protecting all of God's creation. It's an illustration of nature in harmony at the campus as birds and animals have equal rights to the fruits of the trees grown there as the centre staff and visitors.

Fourth, the ECC provides a platform and forum for discussion of unity issues that are relevant to the Indian situation through its programmes and seminars. In these events, it brings together intellectuals, experts and those involved at the ground level in working for a harmonious India. Their deliberations draw media attention and serve to keep wider ecumenism in the limelight.

On another front, the ECC has played the role of an educator. The centre has brought together Indian rural folk, labourers, women and marginalized sections of society and has made them aware of the contemporary situations in which they live. It has also conscientised them about the structures and systems that have misguided and marginalized them. Besides, it equips them to fight for their rights and to live a responsible life in the society.

Sixth, the ECC has been involved in empowerment programmes in Indian villages. It focuses on educating rural children through *balawadis* and on providing health education to the rural poor and medical support through clinics.

SIGNIFICANT CONTRIBUTIONS

ECC's significant contributions to the cause of wider unity in India are not often seen in a spectacular and direct way as it has mainly served as an institution inculcating ecumenical messages in the public. However, its contributions to the cause of wider unity in India are tremendous in an indirect way.

A bridge-builder: ECC has been striving to bridge barriers that divide society on the basis of caste, class, race and religion through its training programmes and seminars. It is not a small achievement when viewed against the experience of ecumenical institutions that were started with great fanfare but became monuments of intellectual sterility and inactivity. ECC has passed the test of time and has contributed significantly to the society particularly as a meeting place of ideas and people. Hundreds of people – young and old, educated and semi-literate, believers, agnostics and atheists – have participated in shaping the concerns of ECC and making it what it is today.

Commitment to Social Amity: The message of peace is not a utopian or abstract theory. But it is a God-given task of all human beings. Peace is the gift of God, but it needs human efforts. ECC is committed to the cause of peace and social amity. In its programme curricula, there is adequate space for responding positively to one's commitment to peace and justice as well as to community building with peace, justice, freedom and dignity.

An incident that happened in 1982 in Kolar district of Karnataka illustrates the ECC founder's commitment to social amity. After a police firing incident. M. A. Thomas personally visited the place, violating police orders and identified himself with the victims. As he was there, listening to the plight of the people, the police firing started again. The police took him into custody for interrogation and later released him. The ECC founder's gesture shows its commitment to peace and justice as well as its message of solidarity with victims of atrocities.

Just and Participatory Society: The ECC's deep commitment to the struggles for a more just and participatory society has challenged people of various backgrounds. The unity that the ECC has been advocating is based on mutual understanding and respect between communities, religions and ideologies. At the same time, it has opposed communal and separatist religious forces.

Ecclesiastical Unity: The ECC has also been committed to the unity of the body of Christ. It has served as a meeting place for all Indian churches, including the Catholic Church. Representatives of churches get to interact with one another and to understand one another. Apart from this, several national and regional consultations on Church unity and related problems have been arranged by the centre from time to time, both at Whitefield and in other places in India.

The conferences served as meeting places for the Roman Catholics and the Protestants for the first time in India. These endeavours of the ECC have been helping Indian churches come closer and discuss pertinent questions in relation to the life and witness of the Church as a whole and in its diverse socio, political, economic, and linguistic contexts.

Life and Ministry of the Church: The ECC has sought to make the Church life and ministry relevant to the people of India and their contexts. The Indian School of Ecumenical Theology was set up as a theological wing of the centre to celebrate the unity in the body of Christ. ISET conferences and seminars have raised many questions on the Church and its mission against the backdrop of the realities in India.

Secularism and Democracy: The ECC is deeply concerned about the democratic future of the Indian State and took the social, economic, political and secular life of Indian people seriously in its mission. And no less a person than eminent Indian jurist, V.R. Krishna Iyer has endorsed ECC's efforts. Talking about ECC, he said: "Our political system will be toned up and our parties will be disciplined by the emergence of this type of movement doing definite good . . ."

Solidarity with the Marginalised: ECC practises its message of solidarity with the marginalised in its staff distribution. About 60 per cent of its staff are drawn from the marginalised dalit and tribal communities and 50 per cent are women. ECC is a community of 90 people, of which 60 people, including children stay in the campus.

Gender Equality: The ECC has sought to spread the message of the need for a society in which all men and women enjoy equal dignity and opportunities. A statement issued by participants of the seminar on 'Women, Development and Peace' organized by ECC from March 19 to 21 says:

> *We affirm that men and women created in the image of God are equal and are stewards of God's creation … we realise that half the world's population are women, who are discriminated on the basis of gender… We recommend that the existing paradigms of development need to be refined towards sustainable development, which would incorporate qualitative approaches from the micro level itself.*

In this respect, ECC has provided emphasis to the Biblical understanding of creation. In God's design, there is no inequality between male and female and thus gender inequality is man-made and we have to work together to improve the same. The centre has given adequate attention in organising programmes that discuss the plight of Indian women in rural and urban settings and has suggested methods for their empowerment.

Social Awareness: The long-term and short-term courses conducted by the National Citizen's Academy and the Vicharodaya College on socio-economic and socio-political issues have helped impart awareness among the people of the problems rampant in Indian society.

Justice and Peace Concerns: ECC's commitment to justice and peace concerns is obvious from the fact that its director is an ex-officio member of the board of directors of Vigil India movement. ECC has access to the villages of India through Vigil India. The connection of ECC to the villages through vigil groups has indirectly helped unite different sections of people at the micro level against human rights violations. Each state has its own Vigil groups and district networks. The impact of such interventions in the Indian villages is reflected in the words of a Vigil group member – a woman in Kanyakumari district, of Tamil Nadu state:

> *"As the people of Kanyakumari district are vulnerable, they must be alert and work for communal harmony with ardent enthusiasm and commitment. The poor people are always the victims of communal riots and not those who instigate the riots. This truth must be carried to every village. We must take a vow to eradicate disharmony between communities and work for the unity of India."*

In the Vigil networks, people learned that communal harmony does not mean mere co-existence of different religions or tolerance of each other. It involves positive interaction between different religious communities, learning from each other's religion, and growing together through active co-operation in building up a new India. In such a situation people would accept each other as brothers and sisters without any mental reservations.

The Vigil India movement has collaboration with the National Human Rights Commission, Amnesty International and other human rights organisations in India and abroad. The ECC indirectly has a network in almost all Indian states that could help it rally masses against oppressive structures and human rights violations.

Environmental Concerns: As a reflection of its commitment to the cause of integrity of creation, the ECC has arranged a plot for ecological education. The variety of trees, plants, herbs, birds, and animals in this plot reminds one of God's beautiful creation and also provides illustrative universal messages of unity. Messages displayed on the trees and posters in the campus remind us of our duty to nature. The *"Eco-Darshan"* study programme helps people identify their involvement in various ways in their respective places.

Ecumenical Connections: The centre has been successful in maintaining a meaningful connection with the Serampore College, the National Council of Churches in India, the Christian Conference of Asia, the Congress of Asian Theologians and the Association of Christian Institutes for Social Concerns in Asia (ACISCA). ECC and ACISCA collaborate and plan their work together. Through ACISCA, the ECC has been in collaboration with all Christian institutes in Asia for social concerns. ECC's association with these ecumenical institutions has been helping the centre to keep its relation with other ecumenical bodies in Asia.

Networking of Experts: The ECC has been serving as an instrument for the networking of experts in the fields of economics, law, science and socio-politics and other professionals. They congregate at the centre to share their ideas in brainstorming sessions that go deep into the contemporary Indian situation. ECC has been successful in building up a think-tank of experts to discuss the relevant issues and concerns of the day.

Self-sustaining Institution: ECC has achieved self-reliance in funds and infrastructure matters over the years, which is a welcome achievement considering the experience of similar institutions in the country. A major criticism against the ecumenical institutions in India has been that they are run by foreign funds. When funds stop flowing, the institution ceases to function.

ECC, however, hardly receives any foreign aid. Careful planning and resource development has brought about financial stability. ECC's experience in this regard could be studied by other institutions with a view to efficiently manage their finances.

ECC has thus made valuable contributions to the cause of the unity of all Indians. Its achievement of self-reliance is an example for all institutions in India. These contributions help people to build the nation based on the values of the kingdom of God.

8

A Perspective for the Future

*All the activities echo the main thrust of the ECC, which is wider ecumenism. One of the challenges we have gained from this ecumenical experience is the realization that we need to uphold the principle of **going beyond** in our life and work – **going beyond** in our understanding of God; **going Beyond** in our relationship with the other, and **going beyond** in our understanding of our very life itself. It is this principle of **going beyond**, which is the need of the hour.*

    – Mani Chacko, *Director of ECC, ECC News, April 2007.*

The Ecumenical Christian Centre is an ecumenical institution in India, established in 1963 by the unstinted efforts of M.A. Thomas. Its major focus was not confined to ecclesiastical unity alone, but was aimed at the unity and empowerment of all people irrespective of religion, caste, culture and ideology. It is an acknowledged fact that the centre has widened the notion of ecumenism by breaking down barriers of caste, colour, and sex and by involving all section of the indian society its programme and activities. So the centre functions not as a religious centre, but as a place for promoting the unity of whole humankind – in every aspect of the its functioning.

The ECC is an offshoot of the paradigm shifts that occurred in the ecumenical movement. By 1961, the ecumenical movement became an expression of Christocentric universalism – the concept that the mission of the Church is not confined to the ecclesiastical realm but also concerns the holistic development and preservation of the whole cosmos in the light of the kingdom values propounded by Jesus Christ. The mission of the Church is considered part of *missio-dei* (mission of God) that is inclusive of the whole humanity.

This newfound emphasis gave priority to the Church as against the earlier focus on missionary agencies in the various mission fields. Prior to the 1950s, the numerical growth of membership in each mission field and mission society had been considered as the primary agenda of mission work, which meant a higher rate of "sheep-stealing" – an informal term that denotes the poaching of the faithful by mission societies. This resulted in the importance of the Church getting diluted and what became relevant was the need to further the harmony between mission agencies and societies.

Gradually, the principle of comity among mission societies in mission fields gained credence as a means of fostering harmony and as part of *missio-dei*.

It then came to be accepted that the Church was the locus of God's mission based on the values of his kingdom. The Church existed, not just for its members, but for the "others" and for the world. The world and its needs, especially in the socio-political and economic realms, were considered part of the Church's mission. Influenced by this thought process, the church got involved in the socio-political struggles of the people in the Afro-Asian countries.

The second Vatican Council also affirmed this position.

This was the ecumenical context that prompted M. A. Thomas to start an institution to meet as far as possible the needs of the people of India for a democratic, social and egalitarian society based on the kingdom values. Besides, India's pluralistic context and religious bigotry in the post-Independence period brought forth the dire need for an institution that could bring together various classes of people to build a just, egalitarian and democratic nation. Being exposed to the religious and secular movements of those times, M. A. Thomas responded by founding the ECC to encourage the unity of all humankind in the efforts to build up a strong democracy. To this end, the ecclesiastical unity among the denominational churches in India was considered a prerequisite.

The ECC dived deep into nation-building concerns in the second-phase when it got involved in various social, political and economic movements that took root in India during the 1970s. The centre was successful in mobilising public opinion against the draconian emergency rule. When human rights concerns in connection with justice and peace came into the world ecumenical realm, the centre responded by founding Vigil India movement and programmes to educate the masses on human rights and justice concerns.

In the 1990s, the centre took up ecological concerns as its main agenda in line with WCC's articulation of the need to preserve God's creation as part of a new wider ecumenism concept.

GLOBALISATION BRINGS IN NEW CHALLENGES

Society evolves over the years and today, ECC must find itself confronted with new challenges in the new globalised world. In today's world, we find expressions and signs of unity in terms of a mono-culture calibrated by market forces. Wealth, meritocracy and technocracy are today's watchwords. These, in turn, are driving the creation of a seamless global community that goes beyond all barriers. Mankind is facing a growing sense of de-spiritualisation as global corporate interests nurtured by transnational corporations and information technology are forging a virtual unity at the cost of God's kingdom values and trampling on traditional localised cultures and languages.

The triumph of the philosophy of globalisation in liberal democracies and free market economies has marginalised the traditional unskilled workers of the world. The world is now focused on mega-scales, leaving in the lurch the common man at the micro-level. Mega-traders, mega-companies, and mega cities are the order of the day ... even mega-churches. The challenge before the ECC is now multifarious, which is to respond to the trends of the contemporary world and to help reinstate the values that have supported mankind.

Contemporary Christianity is diverse, but today the most controversial Christian practice is probably that of proselytism. A wealth-and-health prosperity theology has also come up. For contemporary charismatic Christians, the prophetic and apocalyptical view of the Bible has multiple dimensions. First, end-time prophecy contributes an overwhelming logic and urgency to the matter of conversion and proselytism. The theory goes that since the rupture of the physical world will not occur until all have heard the gospel, Christians must evangelise in order to hasten its arrival.

The prophecy of the second coming motivates people to engage in mission work, but members also use this prophecy rhetorically to convince people that their becoming born again is a matter of some urgency. They use the Bible in a fundamentalist way. A literal application of the Bible, sometimes isolating verses out of context, has distorted the vibrant character of the Word of God. No effort is made to relate the word of God with the challenges and concerns of the context.

In the Indian situation, on the other hand, Hindutva (Hindu-ness) propagandists seek to subjugate and homogenise the ethnic pluralities by establishing the hegemony of an imagined cultural mainstream. This would result in the clash of religions. Both these attitudes – a dominant religious hegemony and Christian "warfare" tendencies – are a threat to religious and racial harmony in the country. The issue of conversion is relevant for Christian denominational churches as well as for other religions. I may be permitted to borrow a framework of analysis of noted theologian and former ECC director K. C. Abraham that reflected on the current situation of India's mainline church denominations.

> *"There are two hegemonies that have nearly total domination of our churches: The first is the hegemony of power, represented by a nexus between ecclesiastical leadership and institutional control ... The other hegemony may be described as the dominance of a charismatic and pietistic spirituality, which is historic and apolitical and has sustained itself by borrowed ideology and spiritual practices."*
>
> – **K.C. Abraham:** *"Transforming Vision"*

The spiritual warfare in contemporary Christianity is more pocketed rather than broader-based. Some of the extremist forms of Christianity teach the converted – predominantly from denominational churches, but also from other religions

– to look down upon, reject or demonise one's own culture. This kind of teaching does not allow any room for commonality, dialogue and fusion. In a globalised world, the "warfare" evangelists have very powerful means of promoting their ideas and shaping developments globally.

There have been accusations from this section that the concept of ecumenism is an attempt to water down the real purpose of mission, as they see it. This has led to these groups terming wider ecumenical movements as "unchristian."

POINTS TO PONDER

Of course, faiths will have intolerant ideas as they pursue certain beliefs and principles, but the real issue is how these ideas are translated into – and managed as – practices and features in public life and in inter-religious relationships. What then are the ethics of promoting one's religion in a multi-religious and multi-racial context? What should be the ethics of challenging the theology, traditions and practices of the historic mainline churches?

Without considering these questions, the groups move forward with their own agenda that endangers even the religious harmony in a pluralistic society.

The ECC, as an institution with wider ecumenism enshrined in its agenda for more than four decades, should bring together leaders of all sections, including the extremist charismatic groups, more meaningfully to discuss, and respond to, the concerns – of the day – especially on the proselytisation issue – both within the churches and with people of other faiths.

On another front, the centre has been capable of promoting the conciliar form of unity in the pluralistic Indian context. The conciliar form of unity does not devalue the ethos of either different Christian denominations or other religions. There is room in this concept of unity for dialogue between Christian denominations and people of other faiths with the ultimate aim of fostering social harmony.

This dialogue has not only brought people of different faiths together, but has equipped them with leadership qualities at the micro level to perpetuate the message of greater unity at the local level. In the Indian context, this is panacea to the nerves frayed by communalist propaganda and religious bigotry. The ECC has been able to help advance secular and 'Kingdom of God' values within India.

However, it could do more to enlighten the churches about their creative role in uniting people of other faiths– or no faith – and ideologies for better living in a sustainable society. And, this could be done through the centre's existing programmes and activities.

It is a recognised fact that the centre took community development as a means to achieve wider unity as well as to declare its solidarity with the defenceless and marginalised communities in India. The institutional expressions of the ECC have helped serve as a conscientiser to the people of India about the country's socio-political and religious conditions and about the need for unity of the whole humankind. Its training programmes has equipped leadership in various areas of the country to work for wider unity of the people. It has also helped to organise a think-tank at the centre and a micro-level network of trainees.

The centre began functioning with the adoption of justice, peace and human rights concerns in its main agenda in the 1970s. During this period, ECC was instrumental in training a number of participants for the cause of human rights and was able to organise vigil groups in every Indian state. It could help provide awareness and guidance to the people towards furthering a secular and democratic society.

The centre included ecological concerns in its agenda in the 1990s. Gradually, an eco-friendly atmosphere was introduced in the ECC campus and all its programmes and training courses started giving attention to the cause of environment protection. Ecological concerns incorporated in its major programmes have been positive gestures towards the goal of larger unity.

FOR A MORE MEANINGFUL EXISTENCE ...

ECC's emphasis on the unity of humankind has been amply reflected in its multi-dimensional programmes. However, to express oneness in God and solidarity with humankind is a hard task and although this is what the ECC aims to accomplish, it has to reflect this vision in its administrative bodies. The structure of these bodies will have to undergo certain changes. The centre should look at bringing people of other faiths and ideologies into these bodies as keeping them away will narrow the centre's vision and commitment. Wider unity in its fuller sense will be achieved only by the participation of Hindus, Muslims and people of other faiths in the centre's General Council and Executive Committee – a significant shift from the present practice of just inviting these groups as special guests at its annual meeting.

As for its programmes, the adage, "what nourishes is not how much food we eat but what we digest", is worth mentioning. What matters is not how many programmes the centre organises, but how much of the programme deliberations and decisions percolate down to micro-levels. The number of programmes and participants in the various programmes organised by the centre have been rising, but it remains doubtful how effective they have been in communicating the message of wider ecumenism to the common folk.

The centre's educational role has also been affected as the duration of the long-term courses have progressively been cut shorter and some of them discontinued altogether. The centre should restart these long-term courses as they were successful in churning out leaders for the cause of wider unity. Perhaps, ECC could look into tying up with some accredited educational body to get these courses affiliated. Such a move will draw more participants as it may open doors for them in churches and the wider society.

ENSURING MESSAGE IS TRANSMITTED

ECC's mobile programmes in different villages have also dwindled in recent times and most of the programmes are being conducted at the centre. But the worth of the programmes has been suspect in the absence of an agency to monitor the participants when they go out to their respective fields of responsibility. This points to the need for a machinery to ensure that the results of the deliberations are not only reported and discussed, but also acted upon by the respective institutions that send their delegates to those programmes.

In addition, the centre has to increase the number of rural mobile programmes so as to strengthen the involvement of the marginalised. The grassroots-level mobilisation of people through mobile programmes and through it, the linking up with localised networks, would help participants relate relevantly to the problems and issues of wider unity of people at the micro levels. So instead of the discussions on the problems at the macro level, it is necessary to continue the emphasis and mobilisation of people in Indian villages for the ECC to realise its vision of wider unity.

Indeed, ECC is not a centre for the elite. The rich and the poor across any class, caste or religious divide attend its meetings. Moreover, most of the centre's staff drawn from neighbouring villages. Dialogues and other consultations with the ECC now appear to take place mostly among the elite. How can the ordinary people be engaged in these dialogues and consultations?

The subjects of dialogue and consultations could be academic or theological. In ordinary life, ordinary people do not usually engage in theological or academic dialogues. Visits of the participants of the centre's programmes to each others' homes and the trickling down of the discussions at these courses to individual homes or localised contexts will provide opportunities for a natural and honest implementation of decisions made at these consultations.

Funds for the day-to-day running of the centre have been raised through proceeds from guest programmes, as it does not depend solely on foreign funds for sustenance. However, due to the high rents at the ECC, common village folk may find it difficult to afford it. There may be a case for the centre to look into raising more funds from member churches and organisations and reduce the burden on the village folk.

STRONGER GRASSROOTS LINKS

ECC has been conducting seminars and conferences both in the campus and outside. The medium of instruction and most deliberations in the centre's training programmes, seminars and conferences is English as the majority of its participants are from English-speaking groups. This means the messages are inaccessible to the common people of India, who live in villages with little knowledge of the English language.

The ECC may thus be open to the charge that it is an ivory tower of experts, intellectuals and academicians. Critics may allege that its grassroots links are not deep, although the centre has been involved in rural empowerment and health programmes.

It's time for the centre to concentrate more on Indian villages than on the elite in cities. In order to achieve this, conferences should be conducted in different languages for people belonging to different regions on a regular basis. In order to maintain solidarity with the ordinary people, the programmes of the centre should concentrate more on the village folk and give importance to their own language.

Apart from these, yet another challenge for the ECC is incorporating polyphonic voices and situations in its programmes to better address concerns of wider unity. This is possible only when the centre widens its village networks by establishing micro level centres of learning with the support and supervision of local people. Such an initiative is bound to help the centre relate relevantly to people's concerns in their own village settings.

The centre needs to resume village development projects like *balawadis*, village clinics, women's empowerment programmes and social emancipation programmes that had worked well earlier.

ECC has succeeded in building up a thinktank of likeminded experts, but rather than remaining at the rhetorical realm, it needs to draw up a considered and well-planned response against social evils like corruption and exploitations in the Indian context. Confining to training programmes and conferences waters down the centre's ultimate task of achieving wider ecumenism. It needs to strongly sustain links with the Vigil India movement and similar action groups towards this end.

ECC's flexibility in policies and its ability to accommodate paradigm shifts in ecumenism are both its strength and weakness. Shifting focus to a particular paradigm should not be at the cost of the other different pillars of wider ecumenism. Equal emphasis should be accorded to the unity of churches, unity of humankind, justice, peace and human rights concerns, and ecological concerns.

UPHOLDING A COSMIC CONCEPT

It is a positive gesture that the centre has taken up as its current challenge a paradigm shift from an anthropocentric to a bio-centric attitude to nature. The ego-centric influential attitude of human beings has placed the whole global community in an alarming situation and we are facing a grave ecological crisis today. The centre's effort to educate the people about the environment as a source base critical for the survival of humankind is indeed praiseworthy.

Still, science is today hogging the limelight and changing our environment. Scientific knowledge has grown by leaps and bounds in the past few centuries and we are fast moving to assumptions that God's handiwork can be manipulated by human mind, disregarding the fact that radical inter-relatedness is the secret of life. The relevance of God in sustaining the cosmos is being ignored. This kind of thinking is against the cosmic concept of wider ecumenism – one family of God under heaven – the fundamental that spurred M. A. Thomas to found ECC.

The progress in life sciences – genetic science, the possibility of human cloning, stem cells and genetically modified food – has posed serious questions regarding the meaning of life to the modern man. Mankind is standing between the belief in God, as the author of life and the sustainer of the cosmos, and a leap in modern scientific enterprise. Modern scientific definitions of life tend to belittle the importance of God and the concept of inter-relatedness in the created order.

The centre has a role to address this issue and communicate the meaning of upholding moral values and the value of inter-relatedness of different species as the basis of the existence of the eco-system. It has the role to educate people to be guarded against a trend to overstate the objectivity claims of modern science as a panacea for all the world's ills.

Critics may also point to the visible domination of a linguistic group in the administrative structure of the ECC in the over four decades of its existence. The centre should find some means to address this criticism to maintain its reputation as a model ecumenical institution.

ECC has come out of a vision – or, a response to a Christ-inspired challenge that M. A. Thomas and other leaders of the centre felt. ECC has to continuously respond to that challenge even as the world hurtles ahead, swayed by the influences of modern times and trampling values, traditions and faiths. In the past, ECC spoke with courage and conviction on national, social, religious, human rights and inter-faith concerns.

The role of ECC must widen by bringing together leaders from different churches and religions more frequently to discuss issues related to wider ecumenism. I hope and pray this study will inspire further studies at the local levels and motivate action.

POLITICAL INVOLVEMENT

ECC had plunged headlong into politics in the 1970s and 1980s. However, there is a felt need in the present times to energise and equip youngsters in the country for a deeper involvement in politics as their interest in nation-building, civil service, and non-governmental organisations (NGOs) has been declining.

Political education may be done at two different levels. The first is at the general citizenship level – that applies to all citizens – and the second at a deeper level of engagement in vocational national citizenship for those challenged by a calling to this area.

General citizenship involves careful and considered voting at election time, engaging with representatives of both panchayats (local bodies) and legislative and parliamentary constituencies through letter-writing, awareness campaigns and occasional meetings. Some may volunteer their spare time to NGOs with social and political goals or join a political party.

At a deeper level, selected citizens trained at the ECC could work full time as politicians, NGO officers, civil-servants, assistants to political leaders, and so on.

To conclude, the story of ECC is the story of commendable efforts to regard all classes of people on equal terms as children of God. The centre as it stands now is a forum to promote religious and political views for the fostering of a just, egalitarian and democratic society in a pluralistic Indian situation. It has played a role in fostering wider unity as well as in energising people for a critical and committed lifestyle in the context of the political, social, economic and pluralistic conditions of India.

ECC's founders and its leaders over the years have built up a strong platform on a vision of a global family. Its relevance in the future will depend on the extent of its resolve to hold fast to that vision and the leadership's ability to translate it to the grassroots.

9
Glossary

Abraham, K.C., Former Director, Ecumenical Christian Centre, Whitefield Bangalore; ecumenical and Third World theologian; director emeritus, South Asia Theological Research Institute (SATHRI), Bangalore; former president, Ecumenical Association of Third World Theologians (EATOWAT); director (research) of the Board of Theological Education of the Senate of Serampore College; former vice-president of the Church of South India (CSI) Karnataka Central Diocese and CSI presbyter.

Arokiaswamy, P., former vice-chairman of ECC and arch bishop of Bangalore

Bonhoeffer, Dietrich (1906-1945), a Protestant theologian executed by Nazis in 1945; deeply-committed German Pastor, scholar and theologian; strong promoter of 'the Confessing Church"; continues to be an inspiration for various Christian communities under political persecution; positive assessment of secularisation as a sign of man's emergence from a self-inflicted, immature dependency on religion is key to his theological discovery.

Chunakkara, Mathews George, former secretary of the Vigil India Movement and former secretary – human rights of Christian Conference of Asia (CCA); currently serving as the executive secretary, World Council of Churches, Geneva, Switzerland; member of Mar Thoma Church.

Chandran, Russel (1918-1999), noted Indian theologian, vice-moderator of the World Council of Churches, 1966-1968; former principal of the United Theological College, Bangalore, India.

Caste System – an Indian social system, whereby one's birth becomes the sole determinant of one's socio-religious position; people divided into groups and classes, each of which with a hereditary occupation and subjected to restrictions on social and religious customs; caste means breed, race or class – a social hierarchy that determines social status of a person in the India social system.

Dalit – an ancient term that's still being used. The root word for *dalit* in Hebrew is *dal* (poor, helpless), which in Sanskrit means to crack, crush, open or split; in popular understanding, the term denotes underdeveloped or backward sections of people such as the Hindu untouchables, or *sudras* (serving caste); the lowest strata in the caste structure of Indian socio-religious life trampled by the upper castes.

Dharmaram Vidyaksetra, Bangalore – an ecclesiastical institution of higher learning, established by the congregation for Catholic Education, Rome, as an independent institute empowered to grant degrees, including Doctorate in Philosophy and Theology.

Ecology – word originating from the science of biology, where it is used to refer to the ways in which living things interact with each other and with their surroundings – air, water, soil, plants, animals, and all human beings come under the ecosystem.

Ezhava – a dominant Hindu community in Kerala, classified under "other backward classes" by the Indian government.

Hargreaves, Cecil, a presbyter and vicar of the Anglican Church, Kent, United Kingdom.

Hindutva – Religiously-motivated social concept, propagated by Hindu zealots as a cultural binding factor, but decried by social analysts as Hindu fundamentalism with political motives.

International Missionary Council (IMC) – An offshoot of the World Missionary Conference held at Edinburgh in 1910, which discovered that the Church is truly a global missionary community with deep roots and a vibrant life in every continent; formed in 1921; IMC Jerusalem meeting in 1928 made the Edinburgh conference message its first consideration, especially in relation to modern secularism; 1938 meeting emphasized the study of the Christian message in a non-Christian world; 1947 Whitby, Ontario IMC set itself to discover the relevance of the gospel to a world recovering from war; 1952 Willingen, Germany stated belief in church unity as an essential condition of effective witness and advance; 1958 Ghana IMC saw the establishment of a theological education fund, providing for substantial aid for buildings, facilities and libraries of institutions in which churches were united in training for the ministry; merged with the World Christian Council at the 1961 WCC New Delhi General Assembly; work continues under the division of world mission and evangelism of WCC.

Joseph, M.J., former director of the Ecumenical Christian Centre, Bangalore; former principal of the Mar Thoma Theological Seminary, Kottayam, Kerala; first registrar of the Federated faculty for Research in Religion and culture (FFRRC) in Kottayam; member of the WCC Faith and Order Commission; former secretary of the Board of Theological Education of the Senate of Serampore College; priest of the Mar Thoma Church.

Kannada – language of the people of Karnataka State, India.

Karnataka – a southern state of India.

Kant, Immanuel (1724-1804), German philosopher regarded as one of the most influential thinkers of modern Europe and the last major philosopher of the Enlightenment; credited with establishing the possibility of objective knowledge of the phenomenal world; his work resulted in experimentation and matter-of-fact observations and marked the start of a leap in science and objective knowledge.

Kerala – a southern state of India.

Kurien, C T., economist and Social thinker; chairman of the Madras Institute of Development Studies; member of the Church of South India.

Malayala Manorama – A regional popular daily in Malayalam.

Malayalam – The language of the people of Kerala.

Mar Chrysostom, Philipose (1918-), twentieth Mar Thoma

Metropolitan who took over in 2000; abdicated the head-of-church status in favour of Joseph Marthoma in 2007; now named "Valia Metropolitan"; one of the great living bishops of Church universal with more than 70 years of ministry behind him; one of the senior-most Church leaders in India; former president of the National Council of Churches; ecumenical leader who has attended the second Vatican Council and several WCC assemblies.

Mar Athanasius, Mathews (1900-1973), former bishop of the Mar Thoma Church; instrumental in establishing educational institutions in the underdeveloped areas of Kerala; established parishes, schools and hospitals in forest areas of central Kerala such as Angamoozhy, Seethathodu, Kochukoickal, Chittar, Malayalapuzha.

Mar Thoma, Yuhanon, (1893-1976), eighteenth Mar Thoma Metropolitan who consolidated the theological and evangelical vision of the Church; pioneer in the Ecumenical Movement; elected president at the 1954 Evanston WCC Assembly (1954); moderator in the WCC Fourth General Assembly in New Delhi (1961); equipped the Church to be sensitive to the needs of the poor and the marginalised; pioneer of the Home for the Homeless scheme, which was later adopted by the Government of Kerala as the "Lakshamveedu Padhhathi" (project for 100,000 homes); vehement critic of social and political evils.

Mithra, Augustine G., director of ECC, 1990-1997.

Nairs – Predominantly middle-class Hindu community, a dominant group in Kerala. They were a prominent political and military class during the time of the Travancore princely state.

Neibubr, Reinhold, a prominent theologian who developed Christian realism in theological thinking; former professor of Applied Christianity at Union Theological Seminary, New York; raised serious questions about the viability of liberal Christianity to meet the intellectual and social realties of the 1930s'; "The Nature and Destiny of Man", written by Neibubr, is one of the most influential books of the last century.

Nellithanam, Sucy, ECC director, 1988-1990.

Nivarthana Prasthanam (1932) – Joint protest movement of the Christian, Muslim and Ezhava communities to eradicate social inequality in the then Travancore state in India; part of the Indian freedom struggle; necessitated by the communal tension in Kerala created by the Civil Disobedience Movement (1930) and the subsequent Abstention Movement..

Oommen, M.A., economist; social scientist; senior fellow, Institute of Social Sciences, New Delhi; former head of the Department of Economics, University of Calicut, Kerala State.

Oslo Conference (1947) – World Conference of the Youth held under the auspices of the World Council of Churches (WCC); held in June 1947.

Synod of Diamper (1599) - A synod of the church called by Menezes, the Arch bishop of Goa and Malabar at Diamper, (Udayamperoor), which is situated five miles south-west of Ernakulam on June 20th, 1959. The synod was an attempt to convert the St. Thomas Christians to Roman Catholic faith. The synod was convened for the increase and the exaltation of the Catholic faith among the Syrians in Malabar; for the destruction of the errors and heresies which had been sown in the dioceses by several heretics and schematics; for the purging of books from the false doctrines contained in them; for the perfect union of the church with the whole church catholic and universal; for the yielding of obedience to the supreme bishop of Rome, universal pastor of the Church and successor in the chair of St. Peter and vicar of Christ upon earth, from whom they had for some time departed; for the extirpation of simony, which had been much practiced in the diocese; for regulating the administration of the holy sacraments of the Church, and the necessary use of them; and for the reformation of the affairs of the Church and the clergy and the custom of all the Christian people of the diocese. Menezes's attempt to convert the St. Thomas Christians to Roman Catholic faith met with strong opposition, especially from the Archdeacon George. But the synod put the St. Thomas Christians under the domination of the Roman Catholic Church that continued for about fifty five years.

Tamil – language of the people of Tamil Nadu, India

Thomas M.M. (1916-1996), noted Asian Christian theologian, prolific writer and social thinker; leader of the ecumenical movement; moderator of WCC Central Committee, 1968-1975; former governor of the Indian State of Nagaland; member of the Mar Thoma Church.

Tomkins, Oliver S., former bishop of Kent and former study secretary of the British Student Christian Movement.

Travancore - A princely state during the British colonial period in the south-west part of India. After the Indian Independence in 1947, it became part of the newly formed state of Kerala (1956).

Vatican Council II (1962-1965) – The 21st Ecumenical Council of the Roman Catholic Church; opened under Pope John XXIII in 1962 and closed under Pope Paul VI in 1965; participated by four future pontiffs – Cardinal Giovanni Battista Montini, who on succeeding Pope John XXIII took the name of Paul VI, Bishop Albino Luciani became Pope John Paul I, Bishop Karol Wojtyla became Pope John Paul II and 35-year-old Father Joseph Ratzinger, the present Pope Benedict XVI; accepted the collegiality of bishops; the "Decree on Ecumenism" a first or the Catholic Church after Reformation; accepted non-Catholic Christian communities in the ecclesiastical sense; a pastoral council which passed sixteen documents emphasising ecumenism understood as religious fellowship, rather than emphasising Catholic missionary enterprise for the conversion to the Roman Catholic faith; no dogma defined and no heresy condemned.

World Council of Churches – Broadest world ecumenical body founded in 1948; brings together more than 349 churches; fellowship of churches on the way to visible unity; may be considered a major river flowing from three tributaries –International Missionary Council, Life and Work Movement and the Faith and Order Movement, all three tracing their source to that epoch-making moment in modern ecumenical history, the 1910 International Missionary Conference in Edinburgh.

10
Appendix

The Rev. Dr. M. A. Thomas
(1913 – 1993)

The Rev. Dr. Madathethu Abraham Thomas was born on August 10, 1913 in Kerala. As a student, he came under the influence of national leaders like Mahatma Gandhi, Jawaharlal Nehru and Jayaprakash Narayan, and identified himself fully with the freedom movement. He graduated from Maharaja's College, Thiruvananthapuram.

Rev. Dr. Thomas entered public life as Secretary of the Inter-Religious Student Fellowship, when the late Dr. S. Radhakrishnan, a great philosopher and former President of the Indian Republic, was the fellowship's all-India president. During 1945-47, he studied at Cambridge, England, and was ordained a priest of the Mar Thoma Church in 1950.

In 1963, he founded the Ecumenical Christian Centre in Bangalore and developed it into a meeting place of people of all religious and political views. The story of ECC is also the story of his commendable efforts to regard all people, irrespective of caste or creed, as the children of one God.

Rev. Dr. Thomas served as Vice- President of the Indian section of Amnesty International (1980-1984); President of the Indian section of Amnesty International (1984-86): the Vice- President of the Association of Christian Institutes for Social Concern in Asia (ACISCA) (1970-74); the President of the Association of Christian Institutes for Social Concern in Asia (ACISCA) (1974-1978). In 1977, he founded the Vigil India Movement, a human rights organization.

Rev. Dr. Thomas authored nine books in English and Malayalam. They include Ormakalilude (Reminiscences) written in Malayalam, Frankly Speaking, Traffic Lights, The Struggle for Human Rights, A Leap into the Unknown, Meditations of an Indian Christian written in English, German and Malayalam, Musings in the Secret Place written in German and English, About You and Me Written in German, English and Welsh and Towards Wider Ecumenism.

He passed away on June 25, 1993 and was interred at the ECC campus.

11
Selected Bibliography

1. PRIMARY SOURCES

A. Books

Gandhi P, Jagadish and K.C. John. *Upon the Wings of Wider Ecumenisam*. Delhi:ISPCK/ECC, 2006.

Iyer, Krishna . *Human Rights –Their Spiritual Dimensions*. Bangalore: Ecumenical Christian Centre, 1996.

Joseph, M.J.   *Vishala Ecumenism* (Malayalam). Tiruvalla: Theological Literature   Council, 1998.

__________. *One in Many and Many in One*. Tiruvalla: CSS, 2005.

Koshy, Ninan. *Religion and Politics*. Bangalore: Ecumenical Christian Centre, 1995.

Kurian, M. A. *Quest for the Unknown*. Tiruvalla: ISPCK/CSS, 2002.

Nellithanam, Sucy. *Ripples-Story of The Ecumenical Christian Centre 1960-1980*. Whitefield: Ecumenical Christian Centre, 1980.

Thomas, M.A. *About You and Me*. Madras: CLS, 1975.

__________. *Frank Speaking, A call to Socio-Political Action*. Bangalore: Vigil India Movement, 1990.

__________. *Ormakaliloode* (Malalyalam). Tiruvalla: CLS, 1984.

__________. *Towards Wider Ecumenism.* Bangalore: Asian Trading Corporation, 1993.

__________. *Traffic Lights.* Bangalore: Ecumenical Christian Centre, 1991.

__________. *An Outline History of Christian Churches And Denominations in Kerala,* Mamacaud: Vijnana Bhavan, 1977.

__________. *Musings in the Secret Place.* Bangalore: Ecumenical Christian Centre, 1992.

__________. *Ormakaliloode* (Malalyalam). Kottayan: Ashram Press, 1984.

__________. *A Leap into the Unknown.* Bangalore: Asia Trading Corporation, 1992.

__________. *Orupothunamam Avasyam Illa* (Malayalam). Kottayam: Palathinkal Press, 1983.

Tides, Visual Story of Ecumenical Christian Centre. Bangalore: Ecumenical Christian Centre,1988.

Van Leeuwen, G, ed. *Worship in Youth Idiom.* Bangalore: Ecumenical Christian Centre, 1988.

Varghese, B.G. *Human Rights, Democracy, Secular and Social Change.* Bangalore: Ecumenical Christian Centre, 1994.

B. Articles

"Are Sermons Cold, Insipid, Moralizing?" *SAP* 1/2 (July, 1968): 1-11.

"Communalism in Indian Politics." *SAP* 1/11 (June, 1974): 1-15.

"Ecumenical Christian Centre Completes Twenty Years." *ECC News* 1/18 (January, 1983): 12.

"Institute on Ecological Concerns." ECC News 1/39 (December, 2002): 5-6.

"Institute on Women's Rights." *ECC News* 3/38 (December, 2001): 19.

"Lack of Efficiency, Loss of Progress." *SAP* 1/6 (August, 1970): 4-15.

Abraham, K.C. "From the Director." *ECC News* 2/19 (June, 1983): 1.

Arokiaswamy. "20th Anniversary Celebrations." *ECC News* 19/6 (June, 1983): 6.

Devadas, E.D." An Interview with Rev. M. A. Thomas." *ECC News 10/2* (August, 1979):5.

ECC News. For the years: 1/1 (January, 1975) - 1/43 (December, 2005).

Fernandes, G. "I Hope that ECC Generates in everyone of us the Capacity to Bridge the Barriers that Divided us." *ECC 2/25* (December, 1988): 14-15,28.

Kottoor, J. "The Ecumenical Christian Centre completes 12 years of Service to Nation," *The South Indian Churchman* 12/1 (January, 1975) : 8.

__________. "The ECC.- An Adventure In Ecumenism." *NCCI Review* XCV/1 (January, 1975): 35.

Nellithanam, Sucy. "Indian School of Ecumenical Theology." *ECC News* 2/24 (December, 1987):3.

Patmury, Joseph. "Reminiscence of a Decade: Ministry of the Indian School of Ecumenical Theology." *Theology for Our Times,* 6/1 (July, 1999): 140.

Theology of Our Times. For the years: 1/1 (July, 1994) - *1/11 (July, 2005).*

Thomas, M.A. "A Personal Experience." *ECC News* 1/17 (July, 1982): 1-2.

__________. "Community Development – New Ventures." *ECC News* 13/12 December, 1980): 7.

__________. "A Recapitulation of Some Events." *Vigil India* 2/42 (June, 1987): 2.

__________. "Community Development – New Ventures." *ECC News* 13/12 (December, 1980): 7.

__________. "Vigil India Peace." *Vigil India* 1/41 (April, 1987): 2.

__________. "Silent Witness." *ECC News* 7/2 (January, 1978): 12.

C. Reports

Ecumenical Christian Centre Office, Whitefield, Bangalore, India. *Report of the Director to the Executive Committee.* For the years: 1966- 2005.

Ecumenical Christian Centre, *Report of the Programme Secretary, National Citizen's Academy.* Bangalore: Ecumenical Christian Centre, 1968.

D. Personal Correspondence

Gandhi, Mohandas Karam Chand. The Father of our Nation. Letter to M.A.Thomas, 21 November 1932.

Thomas, M.A. The founder Director of the Ecumenical Christian Centre. Letter to Yuhanon Mar Thoma Metropolitan, 24 November 1961.

__________. The founder Director of Ecumenical Christian Centre. Letter to Frere Christophe von Wachter, SODEPAX, Ecumenical Centre, Geneva, 7 July 1971.

E.   Unpublished Materials

Thomas, M. A. "The Vision" Manuscript of the Scheme for Ecumenical Christian Center 24th December 1961. Bangalore. Ecumenical Christian Centre Library. Bangalore.

__________. "Manuscript of a President's Address delivered at the National Vigil Workers Meet held at Nagarcoil."1 August 1990. Ecumenical Christian Centre. ECC Library. Bangalore.

II.   SECONDARY SOURCES

A.   Books

Abraham, K.C, ed. *Christian Witness in Society*. Bangalore: Board of Theological Education –Senate of Serampore College, 1998.

Ananthamurthy, U.R. *Would the East and West Meet?* Bangalore: Ecumenical Christian Centre, 1999.

Bonhoeffer, Dietrich. *Prisoner of God.* New York: Harper and Row, 1954.

Chunakara, Mathews George, ed. *Globalization and its Impact on Human Rights*. Hong Kong: CCA & CSS, 2000.

Das, Soman. *Christian Faith and Multi Form culture in India*. Bangalore: UTC, 1987.

Dietrich, Gabriele. *The Impact of New Economic Policy on Women in India And Feminist Alternatives*. Bangalore: Ecumenical Christian Centre, 1997.

Evanston Speaks. Reports from the Second Assembly of the World Council of Churches, August 15-31, 1954. Madras: CLS, 1955.

Fay, Harold E. *The Ecumenical Advance: A History of the Ecumenical Movement1948-1968.* Geneva: WCC publication, 1978.

Fernando, Leonard S.J. *Christian Faith Meets Other Faiths Origin's Contra Celsum and its Relevance to Indian Theology.* New Delhi: ISPCK, 1998.

Gabriele, Dietrich and Bas Wielenga. *Towards Understanding Indian Society.* Madurai: Centre for Social Analysis Team, 1997.

Gill, David, ed, *Gathered for Life: Official Report of VI Assembly of World Council of Churches,* 24 July–10 August 1983, Vancouver, Canada. Geneva: World Council of Churches Publication, 1983.

Goodall, Norman, ed. *The Uppsala Report 1968: Official Report of the Fourth Assembly of the World Council of Churches.* Geneva: WCC Publication, 1968.

__________. *Mission under the Cross.* London: Edinburgh House Press, 1953.

Hogg, William Richey. *Ecumenical Foundations.* New York: Harper and Brothers Publishers, 1952.

Hooft , Visser't W A, ed. *Report of the Amsterdam Assembly of WCC.* Geneva: WCC Publication, 1948.

__________. ed. *The New Delhi Report, the Third Assembly of the World Council of Churches 1961.* New York: Association Press, 1962

Iyer, Krishna. *Human Rights-Their Spiritual Dimension.* Bangalore: Ecumenical Christian Centre, 1996.

Jain, L.C. *Eco Spirituality for Communal Harmony*. Bangalore: Ecumenical Christian Centre, 2003.

Koshy, Ninan. *A History of the Ecumenical Movement in Asia*. Vol.1, China: World Student Christian Federation, Asia and Pacific Alliance of YMCA and Christian Conference of Asia, 2004.

__________. *Religion and Politics*. Bangalore: Ecumenical Christian Centre, 1995.

Kuhn, Thomas S. *The Structures of Scientific Revolution*. Chicago: University of Chicago Press, 1970.

Limourus, Gennadios. ed., *Justice, Peace and Integrity of Creation–Insights from Orthodoxy*. Geneva: WCC Publication, 1990.

Livingston, James C. *Modern Christian Thought* . New York: Macmillan Publishers, 1971.

Massey, James. *Roots- Concise History of Dalits*. New Delhi: ISPCK, 2001.

Meshack, Samuel. *Building God's Kingdom on Earth*. Channai: Gurukul Publication, 1999.

Paton, David M, ed. *Breaking Barriers: Official Report of the Fifth Assembly of the World Council of Churches*, Nairobi, 23 November –10 December 1975. London: SPCK and Grand Rapids, Wm B. Eerdman in collaboration with WCC, 1976.

Paul, Babu. *Festival of Life in the Global Village*. Bangalore: Ecumenical Christian Centre, 2001.

Paulos, Mar Paulos. *Encounter in Humanisation*. Tiruvalla: CSS, 2000.

Philip, T.V. *Edinburgh To Salvador Twentieth Century Ecumenical Missiology*. New Delhi: CSS & ISPCK, 1999.

Premsagar, Victor. *Evangelism Dei: Mission.* Bangalore: Ecumenical Christian Centre, 2000.

Raiser, Konrad. *To Be The Church.* Geneva: WCC Publication, 1997.

__________. *Ecumenism in Transition, A Paradigm Shift in the Ecumenical Movement.* Geneva: WCC Publication, 1989.

Raughly, Ralph C. Jr, ed. *New Frontiers of Christianity.* New York: Association Press, 1962.

Samartha, S.J. *One Christ Many Religions.* Bangalore: SATHRI, 1992.

__________. *Courage for Dialogue, Ecumenical Issues in Inter-Religious Relationships.* Geneva: WCC Publication, 1979.

__________. *Towards a World Community-Colombo Papers.* Geneva: WCC, 1975.

__________. *Between Two Cultures–Ecumenical Ministry in a Pluralistic World.* Bangalore: Asian Trading Corporation, 1997.

Shenoy, P.V. *Markets and Morality.* Bangalore: Ecumenical Christian Centre, 2002.

Singh, K.S. *The Schedule Castes.* New Delhi: Oxford University Press, 2002.

The World Mission of the Church. Findings and recommendations of the meeting of the International Missionary Council, Tambaram, Madras Dec 12-29, 1938. London: International Missionary Council, 1938.

Thomas, K.T. *Judiciary and Social Change.* Bangalore: Ecumenical Christian Centre, 1998.

Thomas, K.V. *Human Rights, Terrorism and Policing in India.* New Delhi: Indian Social Institute, 1999.

Thomas, M.M. *My Ecumenical Journey.* Trivandrum: Ecumenical Publishing Centre, 1990.

__________. *The Secular Ideologies in India and the Secular Meaning of Christ*. Madras: CLS, 1976.

__________. *Towards a Theology of Contemporary Ecumenism- A Collection* of *Ecumenical Gathering (1947-1975)*. Madras: CLS, 1978.

Varghese, B.G. *Human Rights, Democracy, Secular and Social Change*. Bangalore: Ecumenical Christian Centre, 1994.

Vasanthakumar, S, ed. *Call to Ministry and Mission*. Bangalore: The Student Christian Movement of India, 1993.

Williams, Collin. *New Directions in Theology Today: The Church vol. IV*, London: Lutterworth Press, 1969.

Woong, Ahn Jae. *Building a Culture of Peace in Asia Today*. Bangalore: Ecumenical Christian Centre, 2004.

World Missionary Conference 1910. *Report of Commission VIII Co-Operation and Promotion of Unity*. Edinburgh & London: Olyphant, Anderson and Ferrrier, 1910.

Zacharia, Mathai. *Beyond Ecumenism*. Tiruvalla: CSS, 2002.

B. Articles

Arahraja, Wesley S. "Dialogue, Interfaith." *A Dictionary of the Ecumenical Movement*. Edited by Nicholas Lossky. Geneva: WCC Publication, 1991. 281-286.

Bent, Vander Ans. "Ecumenical Conferences." *A Dictionary of the Ecumenical Movement*. Edited by Nicholas Lossky. Geneva: WCC Publication, 1991. 338-325.

Bosch, David J. "Ecumenicals and Evangelicals: a Grouping Relationship." *The Ecumenical Review* 5/3-4 (July-October, 1988): 462.

Dharmaraj, A. C. "A National Consultation of Conciliar Unity." *NCCI Review* 1/CV111 (April ,1978).

Leeming, B. "Ecumenical Movement. " *New Catholic Encyclopedia*. Vol 5 (America: McGrow Hill Book Company,1967): 96-100.

Mendez, Hector. "The Grace of God: Illusion or Reality." *Ecumenical Review* 5/56 (July, 2004): 297.

Mundadan, Mathias. "Emergence of Catholic Theological Consciousness in India." *Documentation No 7, July 1985*. Alwaye: St.Thomas Academy for Research (STAR): 2.

Tavard, George H. "Ecumenism." *The Modern Catholic Encyclopedia*. Edited by Michael Glazier. (Bangalore: Claretian Publication, 1994):272-275.